MW01000361

# BE... DON'T DO.

## THE SHERPA GUIDE TO
## COACHING FOR MANAGERS

**BRENDA CORBETT & JUDITH COLEMON**

# BE... DON'T DO

Brenda Corbett & Judith Colemon

SECOND EDITION
Revised and copyright 2014 by
Sherpa Coaching - Cincinnati, Ohio USA

Based on the executive education course "Coaching Skills for High Performance" Developed by the authors at Penn State, and taught globally, on site and on campus.

"Coaching Skills" programs can be arranged directly with the authors. They are available to travel for on-site delivery, as they have done for The Human Genome Research Institute, L'Oreal, Toyota, US Bank and many others.

Printed by Pocket-Pak, The Colony, TX
www.pocketpak.com

Distributed by Sasha Corporation
Cincinnati, Ohio, USA

This publication is designed to provide accurate and authoritative information on the topic covered. It is made available with the understanding that the publisher is not offering legal or other professional advice. If expert assistance is required, you should seek the services of a competent professional.

Unless otherwise specified in the text, no part of this publication may be copied or transmitted by any information storage or retrieval system without permission from Sherpa Coaching.

For more information about Sherpa Coaching's services and products, contact:

Sherpa Coaching          (513) 232-0002
PO Box 417240, Cincinnati, Ohio 45262
info@sherpacoaching.com
www.sherpacoaching.com

Copyright notice: The leadership training material and techniques contained herein and use of the term Sherpa, as applied to executive coaching and leadership development, are the intellectual property of Sherpa Coaching, LLC and the authors, and copyright 2002-2014.

The purchaser and/or reader of this book is encouraged to apply the techniques described in their management of people in for-profit, non-profit, government and educational settings.

The authors reserve the right to teach, or license others to teach, any publicly-offered course or program based on the book, and grant no such licensing or rights by publishing this book.

Single copy and bulk purchases of this book can be made on line at the authors' on line store, with quantity discounts available. Three related DVD's are also available.

To order, please visit:
www.sherpacoaching.com/store

# Dedication

This book has been written with gratitude

for the support of Certified Sherpa Coaches

around the world.

It is the result of our rich experiences

with managers and executives who have trusted us

with their careers, and had the courage to change.

# Table of Contents

# Introduction

## Be... Don't Do: What does that really mean?

We work with leaders: supervisors, managers and executives. We hear about the challenges of their working lives. They tell us everything.

Most of a manager's life is about doing things. Completing tasks. Getting results. Doing is rewarded. It is easier to do, instead of leading and motivating *others* to do things.

What if you slowed down and concentrated on how you should *be*?

Let our team of Sherpa coaches help you work on being a leader. Over many years, we have mastered the art of being, and we are going to teach you... how to *be*, instead of just *doing* as a manager.

Ultimately, *being* will help you *do* more effectively.

## BE more aware. BE more present. BE more you.

If you want to be a successful manager at any level, you'll need to know that it is impossible to succeed just by doing. If you want an organization that lasts, an organization that has life, you must know who you are as a leader.

*Be* and *do* are dependent on each other. As you think about results, you must make sure your people perform, while they succeed as human beings.

Managers that tap into peoples' hearts will build lasting relationships as they get things done. It is important that you learn how to both *be* and *do*. This book will help you work on the being side of your job and in the process, help your doing side.

- **BEing means giving up ownership:** You are not responsible for everything that happens. At the same time, you are responsible for the end result. To truly *be*, you have to let go of work that needs to be done by your people. You have to recognize those times when you don't need to do the work yourself, even if you can do it better.

- **BEing means listening:** You hear the words, you hear the meaning, and you hear what the person in front of you is truly saying. You stop jumping to conclusions and inventing what people are saying; just listen and *be*.

- **BEing means asking questions:** Clarify and define information your people need. You engage people in the conversation and allow them to be heard and noticed.

- **BEing means setting expectations:** You are not doing the work; you are coaching your people to clearly hear you and do what they need to do.

- **BEing means using coaching moments:** This effectively stops you from solving, solving is doing. You are going to have to solve problems that are your job, but you don't have to solve problems that aren't yours. You don't have to do it all.

# What to expect from this book

You already know what to *do*. We will teach you how to *be*. This book will teach you how to be a more effective leader. This book will add coaching to the range of skills you bring to your job. There are four parts to this journey:

- **We'll take a good hard look at *you*.** We will look at your strengths and weaknesses. We will find out what really motivates you. When we're done, you'll understand how these things play out in your working life.

- **We will make communicating with your people easier and simpler, every time**. You will accomplish this by setting expectations the Sherpa way. You will be given steps to make sure people always hear you. You will be given a process that simplifies your job... and makes sure people always know what you want.

- **We will give you a toolbox**. Your toolbox will be filled with ways to handle difficult situations. One of your biggest obstacles is understanding what to do when you have a problem person on your team. We are here to give you a helping hand.

- **We will help you create and sustain change.** You will learn a simple technique called QUESTION that puts your goals to the litmus test. Apply it effectively, and your coaching skills will stand the test of time.

Be... Don't Do is designed as a quick read, and as a career companion. Read the book straight through, until you get to the questions in Chapter 6. From there, you will have all our tools and techniques in context. Then, you will know exactly how this book applies to your working life, and how to use it as a desktop companion going forward.

# This One's for You

This book is for you: the executive, the leader, the manager. If someone works for you or reports to you, if others look up to you, this book has been written for you. It is used in executive education classes all over the United States, but it has no boundaries. It works anywhere in the world.

We have worked with executives and managers from six continents. We have learned that human nature is universal. People behave in the same ways all over the world. No matter where you were born, where you live, human nature is something we all have in common.

You might challenge this by thinking: '*You don't know me. You don't know where I came from. You don't know what works for me.*' Actually, every person we have ever taught has quite a bit in common. Our similarities outweigh our differences.

We have seen people take chances to reach a personal summit. This book is about that journey. You are about to travel to places where you have never been. Pack your suitcase, fasten your seat belt and enjoy the ride.

This book is a journey, and it leads to what we call your 'personal summit.' Like Sherpa mountain guides, we will lead you to the top, whatever your summit may be. Each part of the book has three activities for you to practice and work through.

**1.  Develop Your Coaching Skills:**
Assessments, activities and exercises to help you use what you have just learned. Some of these will take time; others can be done in the moment. These exercises are the equivalent of the homework we give to our coaching clients.

**2.  How To Use This Tool:**
Practical ideas about the coaching tool you have just studied, including a case study and description of how to use the coaching tool we have described. This section will include case studies which fall under the heading 'Stories From the Summit.'

3.  **Sherpa Words:**
Specific words, sentences and questions that help managers get the most out of the tool or technique we are discussing. People tell us that self-help books tell you what to do, but don't tell you how to do it, especially what to say when a situation arises. Here, we solve that problem.

This book will help you enjoy your role as a manager more. It will teach you to be a coach. It will help you deal with difficult situations, using tips, tricks and techniques that might be new to you. If you already use these techniques, this book will remind you of the value and importance of continuing to use them.

This book promises to make your job easier. We know we can't take that difficult person off your hands, but we can give you the right words for dealing with them. We will teach you simple steps that will help you through the hardest part of being a manager. We will help you look at management in a different way, a more proactive way... a coaching way.

To start our journey, think about these questions:

- What led you to be a manager?
- What do you like most about being a manager?
- What is exciting about your job?
- What is unique about your job?
- What do you do best in your job?
- How well do you know yourself?

If we ask you to describe yourself in your role at work in a 30 second commercial, what would you say? How would you describe what you do?

Let's start thinking about you, and what motivates you as a manager. You can't begin your journey to *being,* without a starting point. That starting point has to include the right mindset. Let's start with a commercial, a verbal message that concentrates on your best traits for 30 seconds.

Here is how to write a 30-second commercial about yourself.

Think through these questions:

- What are my strengths?
- What do I love about this job?
- What is the foundation of my management style?
- What do I find important about what I do?

Introduce yourself to the world. Write a script to describe the most important features that you want your boss and peers to know about you. Include your skills, strengths, and talents. Read your script out loud and time yourself. Thirty seconds is all you have.

Here is one example:

> *I love what I do. My name is Larissa. I manage a beauty salon. I call the women who work for me 'my girls.' They are so supportive and involved in the growth of Clip Company. I am constantly amazed that I can manage a salon and also take care of my own customers. I love the fact that my customers keep coming back. I see return customers at all of my girls' stations.*
>
> *Talk about a successful business. No matter what's going on in my customers' lives, I provide a getaway. I have women come up to me and thank me for the salon, thank me for the music and the peace they feel. Yes, my salon. I am thrilled that I can do that for people.*

The 30-second commercial helps you acknowledge your worth, your importance, and your uniqueness. It is a beautiful way to start your journey. Memorize your commercial. Practice it on friends and family. After all, it's only 30 seconds. You have time to say it, and they have time to listen.

# Chapter One
# The Sherpa in You

**The Sherpa**

In the Himalayas, the native guides that assist climbers to the top of Mount Everest are called Sherpas. The role of the Sherpa, leading and guiding, is very much like your job as a manager or as an executive. We have interviewed Sherpas who have been to the top of Everest, and distilled their wisdom into practical business terms. Here's what we learned:

**Sherpas are the best at just 'being'.** They live in their role as the guide who gets climbers to the top of the mountain. In the thin air on Mount Everest, doing too much will waste precious energy. 'Being' helps you do just what you need to do to reach your goal: put one foot in front of the other. Don't do too much, and don't over-think things. "Be where you are, otherwise you will miss your life." This is the truth they live by, and what they teach climbers as well.

**Sherpas lead others up a mountain.** Though everyone knows the challenge of the mountain and the work involved with the climb, not everyone climbs in the same way. The Sherpa needs to know the true path, so everything else can fall into place. They can only do this by being constantly present. To *be...* is to be present.

**Sherpas are advisors.** They assist each team in getting successful outcomes and conclusions. Sherpas offer up ideas, experience and directions, but allow the team to choose how they will approach the climb.

**Sherpas are guides**. They get their people to their highest performance by knowing the terrain and understanding what must happen in order for people to reach the summit.

**Sherpas are facilitators.** They allow climbers to reach the summit through their own skill and determination. Climbers have to do things for themselves. The Sherpa is only there to guide the process.

The Sherpas of Nepal are masters at what they do. This book will help you acquire their strengths as a manager. We are going to help you be an advisor, be a guide and help those around you reach a personal summit. We are going to help you become a coach, a Sherpa coach.

Being a Sherpa coach takes time and understanding. Coaching will make your job easier and allow you to be the best you can be; surrounded by people who clearly understand you and their job.

The Sherpa on the mountain provides equipment, supplies and recommendations for climbers. Each climber then decides what to use, what to carry and what to do. Just like the Sherpa, we will provide you with all kinds of tools, examples and ideas. Some will work for you, some may not. The key for you is to try them all, and embrace what works for you.

---

### Definitions

**Manager:** From this moment on, we will use the term 'manager' when we talk about all executives and leaders: supervisors, directors, vice presidents, and presidents. The intent is simply to have a uniform designation for your role. Simply put, if people report to you, you are a manager.

**Direct report:** Your staff, the people you are responsible for, the person who reports to you, the people under you on the organizational chart. We use the term 'direct reports' for your workforce, your labor pool, or your employees.

**Boss:** Your direct supervisor, whoever that may be: department head, board, vice president, CEO, unit manager, administrator or executive director.

---

### What is a Manager?

A manager is someone in charge of one or more people, whose success comes from creating efficiency and reliability in deliverables and due dates.

Here are some other characteristics of the manager's role:
- Senior to subordinate
- Provides necessary information
- Meets performance measures
- Responsible for reliable results
- Solves problems
- Creates tactics or strategies

Please write down a few functions and characteristics of your job:

_____

_____

_____

_____

_____

_____

Managers have a critical role. They keep things moving and make sure results are exactly where they should be. At the same time, they must make sure their direct reports learn, advance, enjoy and participate in their work.

By far, a manager's most difficult task involves dealing and working with people. This can be difficult, because every person in the workplace has different needs, values and goals.

No matter how many people you direct, you have to know how to appeal to each person's needs, wants and desires. Failure to do so can affect whether or not tasks are done properly, on time, or at all.

Sherpa coaching skills will help you deal with your people. You will have all you need to experience your job in a new light.

**As a manager, your success is based on the success of your direct reports.** If you are able to create and sustain an environment in which your people succeed, their success comes back to you.

**The Manager's Hats**

Managers can wear many hats. Some of those hats might include the following:

- Team leader
- Visionary
- Problem solver
- Decision maker
- Goal setter
- Cheer leader
- Defender

Sometimes, coaching is another one of those hats a manager wears.

We split the manager's hat right down the middle, giving equal time and importance to managing and coaching. Your role as a coach is just as critical as your role as a manager.

No matter what the situation, you can put coaching skills into play. You can learn how to work with tasks and people at the same time. Managing is best suited for dealing with tasks. Coaching is best suited for dealing with people. We are going to teach you new ways to deal with people, so you will always have a coaching side on your hat.

---

**What is Coaching?**

From now on, we will call you a coach, and focus on developing your coaching skills. A coach is someone responsible for drawing out new behaviors in staff and colleagues. The coach's success comes from helping individuals overcome limiting behaviors and habits that affect their ability to work with others.

In this book, we teach you how to coach for better behavior, skillfully dealing with people's actions and reactions.

**What are the Benefits of Coaching?**

**1.   Clarity:  Communication improves.**
When we are caught up in *doing* all day, communication takes a back seat.  Coaching brings it front and center and makes it a critical component of your day.  We will spend a lot of time in this book discussing communication techniques.

**2.   Teamwork:  Managers and direct reports work through difference and pull together.  Accountability soars.**
Increased teamwork is always a plus.  Work becomes easier when everyone contributes.  Coaching ensures that responsibilities are communicated clearly to each team member.

**3.   Focus:  Managers direct attention to issues, avoid negative emotions.**

Negative emotions should not get in the way of decision making.  We want to help you focus on significant situations and the issues related to them.  Sticking with issues is often difficult because feelings can get in the way.  When feelings are involved, people often say things they later regret.  This needs to stop. We will provide the how-to when addressing negative emotions.

**4.   Morale:  Managers understand direct reports' motivations.**

Understanding your people is critical to your success.  When you don't take time to know your people and what drives their behavior, morale suffers.   Providing recognition takes work.  You can offer recognition simply by communicating clearly and asking good questions.  We'll show you how.

**5.   Leadership: Managers stop 'owning' things they should not own.**

The ultimate *do* in management is ownership. As a manager, you tend to own everything that is placed in front of you.  There's a problem with that.  The more you own, the less you can *be* a manager.  You get caught up more with *doing* than *being*.  How do you let go?  Through empowerment.  We'll show you how.

**Empowerment is one of the toughest concepts for a manager to embrace.**

Empowerment means placing ownership with your direct reports. This is where it needs to be. This means delegation: being able to let your employees take control of the things they are supposed to work on.

When you empower a direct report, you don't take on another task. Instead, you teach your direct report that it is *their* task to deal with... and you make them comfortable dealing with it.

---

**Stories from the Summit:**

*Danielle is a busy manager at a retail store. She is into everything related to her sales staff. One day, as Danielle sits in her office, Nora walks in, saying: "I don't know how I'm going to make my house payment."*

*Danielle swings into action, thinking out loud, figuring out exactly what steps Nora should take to make the payment. Nora just sits quietly as Dani rambles on. She doesn't even take any notes. After 15 minutes, Nora leaves, having said very little.*

*Danielle spent 15 minutes on a topic that has nothing to do with her own job or Nora's job. Nora left, perhaps a little less burdened, but nothing was solved. Danielle took ownership of the problem. Had she left the ownership with Nora, and gotten Nora more involved in the conversation, perhaps something good might have happened. As it was, nothing happened, beyond two people wasting 15 minutes of their time.*

---

Many managers get stuck by owning things when they need to BE. We are going to help you get unstuck. If you are truly going to BE a manager, then owning everything is not part of your life.

## Being, not Doing

Usually, you read Dos and Don't Dos in a book like this. That's not our primary focus. Ours is to help you *be* much more than *do*. Here are some helpful hints:

**BE** reflective. Reflection requires that you step away from noise. Finding peace and quiet might require you to spend more time alone. Through reflection, you will be able to stop running, stop doing things, and find some truths about yourself.

### DEVELOP YOUR COACHING SKILLS

As you go through these questions, reflect. Fill in the appropriate answers in the column labeled "Where I am now." Then, go back through the questions and fill in the column labeled "Where I would like to be." Remember, you are comparing your current situation with the ideal.

| 1 = Almost never    2 = Some of the time<br>3 = Most of the time    4 = Almost always | Where I am now: | Where I'd like to be: |
|---|---|---|
| I find myself saying: 'I don't have time.' | | |
| I make time on the weekends to re-group. | | |
| I continuously go from one activity to the next during the week. | | |
| I take care of everyone except myself. | | |
| I know how important it is to stop and think about life... and I do it. | | |
| I know what the important people in my life really think of me. | | |
| I enjoy anticipating my next vacation. | | |
| Reflecting is part of my life every day. | | |
| I enjoy each day. | | |

- Find a couple of statements where your answers are different by two or three point values. Reflect on these statements and examine how you can get where you'd like to be.

- When you are constantly doing, you do not reflect. This is the first tool you can add to your coaching toolbox. Take time to reflect. Make time to reflect.

## BE relaxed:   Enjoy your work.

Enjoy your direct reports.  Sit back and listen to them.  Don't think you have to provide every answer. You don't.  Most times, a direct report will come up with answers on their own.  You are a guide, a facilitator.  You are someone he can bounce things off.  The more relaxed you are, the more you listen, the better prepared you are to help your direct reports.

What does it look like when you are relaxed during a work day? What can you do to create a relaxing atmosphere and comforting environment?  How can you create a place where people are not afraid to speak up, a place without anger, a place where work gets done and people enjoy doing it?

### DEVELOP YOUR COACHING SKILLS

- On a scale of 1 -10, how do you rate your workplace as a relaxed environment? (1 – never true, 10 – always true)

| | |
|---|---|
| We have comfortable chairs and couches. | |
| The colors are pleasant and restful. | |
| There is easy access to dining areas and space to talk. | |
| Laughter is heard in the halls. | |
| There is lots of space. Nothing is cluttered. | |
| We have plants and personal items in our work areas. | |
| We have our area organized and looking the way we want it to. | |
| There are few arguments and angry words. | |
| People have 'favorite things' around. | |

If you have less than 10 in any area, you have room for improvement. Can you change something? Could a more relaxing environment benefit you and your team?

## BE knowledgeable about your people.

People don't care how much you know until they know how much you care. How do you connect with your direct reports? Coaching will connect you with your people comfortably. Just be around them. Learn about them; learn about who they are, and what makes them tick.

### DEVELOP YOUR COACHING SKILLS

Practice the mantra: "People don't care how much I know until they know how much I care."

Answers these questions about you:
- Do your people really know you?
- Do you really know your people?
- Do you have an interest in getting to know them more?
- Do you see the value in knowing your people?

## BE a coach every day. Create new habits.

This whole coaching thing takes practice. Sure, you can learn to say the words fairly quickly, but living it and using it brings it to life.

**We have talked about four coaching BE's:**
- **Be reflective**
- **Be relaxed**
- **Be knowledgeable**
- **Be a coach every day.**

15

There are also things you should not do. We call them Coaching DONT's.
Let's look at a few:

# ... **DON'T** be afraid to make time for coaching.

In the beginning, you may think coaching takes too much time. Actually, you don't
have time <u>not</u> to do this. You have to be willing to spend time on the front end to
have success on the back end.

How do you look at time? Do you feel as if you don't have enough of it? Think
about the role time plays in your working life. Get ready to make an investment.

## DEVELOP YOUR COACHING SKILLS

Answer these questions about your work:

- Can you tell when things are truly urgent?
- Do you have an hour each day for reading, planning or creating?
- How much time do you spend developing relationships with direct reports?
- Are you often distracted? What distracts you?
- What's the most productive time of day for you?

Review your answers and see if you are happy with them.

- What question should you re-visit?
- What area needs further work?
- How can you make sure you are using your time wisely?

A perceived lack of time gives you an excuse not to do the coaching you should do.
If you examine time now, you will not have issues with it later as you begin to coach.

16

# ... **DON'T** let situations go unresolved.

Do you have a history of avoiding problems?  Do you walk the other way when someone you should deal with approaches?  Do you run from conflict or confrontation? Coaching can help.  You will be given the words to deal with the tough situations.

## DEVELOP YOUR COACHING SKILLS

Answer yes or no to the questions below:

- I evaluate a problem quickly and solve it immediately.
- I deal with confrontations when they arise.
- I deal appropriately with conflict.

If you answered no to any of these questions, developing your coaching skills will make you more effective as a leader.

# ... **DON'T** talk too much.

Do you talk too much?  Have you used too many words to get out of a situation?  Use the 3-Sentence Rule, something we'll teach you later on.  One of the most consistent rules for success in communication is brevity.  We want to make sure you are always listened to.  The 3-Sentence Rule is a good start.

# ... **DON'T** give all the answers.

Be clear about your role, in your own mind and with your direct report. Direct reports will often ask their manager to produce the solution to a problem. Your first instinct is most likely to find answers and solve problems. Instead, ask questions, then more questions.

Your role, as a responsible coach, is to foster independence. To work on this, ask your direct report to find the solution on his own, if at all possible. Guide, without offering ready-made scenarios. The results will surprise you. This is often a difficult area if you, as a coach, are prone to problem solving. Don't go for the quick fix.

---

We have talked about four coaching DONT's:
- **Don't be afraid to make time for coaching**
- **Don't let situations go unresolved.**
- **Don't talk too much.**
- **Don't give all the answers.**

Review the last few pages and ask: How well are you doing with all of this? Personally rate your comfort level with each one of these concepts, on a 1-10 scale.

(1 – This is really tough, 10 – I find this easy.)

| Coaching BEs | My Score |
|---|---|
| Reflect | |
| Relax | |
| Understand your people | |
| Practice | |

| Coaching DON'Ts | My Score |
|---|---|
| Don't be afraid to use the time you need. | |
| Don't let a situation go unresolved. | |
| Don't talk too much. | |
| Don't always give the answer. | |

How hard will it be to attain the BEs and avoid the DON'Ts?

Capture your thoughts:

_____

_____

_____

_____

# Chapter Two
# What makes a good coach?

As you become a coach, we'd like you to know what it takes and what you have to work on to make this transition. In our book *The Sherpa Guide: Process-Driven Executive Coaching* we discuss ten qualities that make a good full-time executive coach. For the coaching manager, we clearly identify three qualities that stand out as the most important.

**Here are the top three behaviors, skills that help you become a coaching leader:**

1. **BE a good listener**
2. **BE inquisitive: ask great questions**
3. **BE objective and centered: remove your filters**

You must have, or develop, these skills to be an effective coach. Let's take a look:

**Coaching Skills (1 of 3):  BE a good listener**

All coaches benefit from good listening skills. If you're a big talker, love to tell stories and be the center of attention, curb those tendencies when you coach. If you get easily bored listening to people's stories, you'll have to work extra hard to be a coach. Coaches are great listeners. That means more than hearing and understanding. In the dictionary, listening is defined as "the conscious effort to hear." We'll show you how.

---

**Stories from the Summit:**

*Jenny wanted to be a good coach.  She was an enthusiastic, high-level manager of 20 years. Jenny took on the challenge of coaching and failed.  Her direct reports did not like the way she approached their coaching moments.*

*They were ready to share the details of their day, and wanted Jenny to hear them. Jenny could not keep her life out of the conversation.  She would constantly say: "That reminds me of something that happened to me..." The direct report would always lose the spotlight. Jenny overwhelmed the conversation.  She needed to stop talking about herself, and really listen to them.  But Jenny never mastered the skill. She thought it was just too much work.*

---

## How are you as a listener?

Think carefully about each question. Review the way you feel and the way you act, and then write your answers (1, 2, 3 or 4) in the right hand column. Your total score provides an important gauge of your listening skills.

| When listening, I do the following:<br><br>1 = Almost never    2 = Some of the time<br>3 = Most of the time    4 = Almost always | My Score: |
|---|---|
| 1. I pay attention, even when I am not interested in a topic. | |
| 2. I wait for speakers to finish before evaluating their messages. | |
| 3. I listen for feelings as well as subject matter. | |
| 4. I stop myself from interrupting the person speaking to me. | |
| 5. I listen to people, even though I have no personal interest in them. | |
| 6. I am aware of my own body language as a listener. | |
| 7. I work to make myself really want to listen. | |
| 8. I maintain emotional control, no matter what is said. | |
| 9. I would rather listen than talk. | |
| 10. I am good at summarizing what someone has just told me. | |
| **TOTAL SCORE:** | |

## What Your Score Means:

**34-40 - *You are an exceptional listener.*** Remind yourself to <u>stay that way</u>. Can you identify, as a coach, when you lose concentration? Do you recognize and pull back from moments when you are not paying attention? Does your lack of focus have to do with a certain topic or person? You need to know yourself well, so that red flags go up in those situations.

**26-33 - *The mark of a good listener.*** Stand back and watch yourself more carefully. What questions pulled your score down? On which questions did you give yourself a '3' or less? Revisit those questions and see if you can figure out what really happens to you in those situations. What is it that distracts you? What makes you lose interest?

**21-25 - *You're a fair to poor listener*** - Allow more listening time in your conversations. You don't want a score in this range if you are serious about coaching. You are easily distracted, and just as interested in talking as you are in listening.

**20 and below – *You have listening problems.*** Develop your skills. Think things through. Practice new behaviors and retake this test in ten days.

**Learning how to listen is very important if you are going to be a good coach.** Here's a tracker for your listening skills to help you evaluate a single conversation. Make copies, if you like. Remember to actively listen during the entire conversation with each direct report.

In fact, there are three times that make up the behavior of an effective listener:

1. **Before a meeting**
2. **During a meeting**
3. **After a meeting**

Let's get familiar with a three-point checklist that helps you cover: **Before, During and After** in a way that makes you a better leader.

1. BE a good listener. **Before** meeting with a direct report, ask:

How do I avoid acting on preconceived notions? How can I stop jumping to conclusions? How do I stay clear and open? How can I listen and just *be*?

_____

_____

How do I ensure that I am actively listening? Jot down some reminders:

| Body Language | How well do I do this? | What do I need to work on? |
|---|---|---|
| Lean in slightly as someone speaks. | | |
| Nod the head to show agreement. | | |
| Make eye contact. | | |

2. BE a good listener. **During** the meeting:

| How did I handle this meeting? | Scale (1-10) | How do I know? |
|---|---|---|
| I did not jump to conclusions. | | |
| My direct report knew I was truly listening. | | |
| I could identify important words in the conversation. | | |
| My emotions were left out of the conversation. | | |
| My body language lent itself to listening. | | |

3. BE a good listener. **After** the meeting:

| Areas to watch for next time: | Scale (1-10) | How do you know? |
|---|---|---|
| Did I miss opportunities to learn? | | |
| How successfully did I avoid distractions? | | |
| Was I able to stay in the moment? | | |

So, our first coaching skill is: being a good listener. Once you know how to listen, it's important to get the best possible information coming your way. That leads us to our next coaching skill.

**Coaching Skills (2 of 3): BE inquisitive. Ask great questions.**

---

**A coach is inquisitive:** Asking questions shows people that you care. It's an art. It takes work. Asking questions is the way to be inquisitive.

Being inquisitive:
- *engages others.*
- *allows you to listen more effectively.*
- *empowers your people.*

Most of all, asking questions shows respect, invites dialogue and helps everyone find the source from which answers come: within themselves.

As a coach, use questions such as:
- *What do you mean?*
- *Can you explain that in more detail?*
- *Can you re-phrase that for me?*
- *How could you have handled that differently?*

An inquisitive nature, really wanting to know more, creates a learning environment for your direct reports. People notice that, and it makes a big difference to your relationships.

---

**Stories from the Summit:**

*Dana came to her manager and said "I have too much to do. I can't get it all done. There is no way I can finish this project on time. I am just overwhelmed."*

*Dana's manager, Erin, answered by asking these questions:*
*"Let's look at the options. Step back and look at the work you have to do. What is due first? What is due next? Who can help you?"*

*Dana looked at Erin and said: "This is the first time I have stopped to see what is going on. Thank you. I will prioritize the work and get Martha involved in a more constructive way. I really appreciate the time you spent with me to work this out."*

---

**Coaches who are inquisitive ask questions until their direct report can reach a satisfactory answer on his own.**

As a coach, you are a facilitator: one who makes it easy for the direct report to reach their own conclusions. How do you draw a direct report out? With questions. Framing an effective question is an important skill, one of the most important components of coaching.

You don't have to say much more than "What is that about?" and wait for a response. Don't provide the answer. *Be* there to provide the right question. That is truly your job as a coach. As we learn this coaching skill, asking great questions, let's explore a few guidelines that will make it easier.

---

**Five Guidelines for Asking Great Questions**

Here we offer guidelines that help you ask the right questions, and only the right questions, at the right time. When you do that, you clear the way for your direct report's self-discovery.

---

Asking Great Questions: Guideline One:
**Don't ask a question unless you <u>truly</u> want an answer.**

---

**Stories from the Summit:**

*Diane loves to talk to everyone at work about what she does over the weekend, especially the time she spends with her grandchildren. It doesn't get in the way of her work. However, give her an opportunity to talk about her weekend, and you will have trouble stopping her.*

*Katie is her manager. Katie needs some overtime work on a special project that is going to require some weekend hours. Katie knows that Diane is the best person for the job. She approaches Diane, and the first question she asks is: 'What are you doing this weekend?'*

---

Think about Katie's question for a moment: Is that the question Katie should be asking? We are going to say, "No." Diane will start a long story about her grandchildren before her boss can get a word in edge-wise.

What happens? Katie's request, because it follows Diane's weekend story, loses its importance.

**Consider (for Katie):** *I have a special project that is important, Diane, and you are the best person for the job. Could you come in Saturday from 10-3 and complete it?*

We are not saying that you should ignore Diane's needs. We *are* saying you should be mindful of the answer you really want before you ask a question.

As managers, we keep getting in too deep. When you are learning to ask questions, follow this rule:

25

**Don't ask a question unless you truly care and need to have an answer.**

Here's what can happen when you do not follow this rule:

1. You shut down and stop listening.
2. You look like you don't care. People take that personally.
3. You have trouble getting to the point.
4. You end up wasting time.

---

**Stories from the Summit:**

*Shirley is a direct report who has lots of stories, especially about her dogs. She usually comes into your office with a story every Monday morning.*

*You have an urgent project that needs to be discussed this morning and don't want her stories to get in the way. It is important that you stay connected to her, but you don't want to waste time hearing about dog training. What do you ask?*

*Scenario A:*

*Shirley says: I had a great weekend with Spike, he learned all kinds of things.*
*You ask: What did Spike learn?*

*Scenario B:*

*Shirley says: "I had a great weekend with Spike, he learned all kinds of things."*
*You ask: "That's great, Shirley! (pause) I have an urgent project that we need to discuss this morning. Do you mind if we get started right away?"*

---

Does Scenario A work? Do you care, or have any desire to know what Spike learned? Do you have a mandated need to know this for the betterment of your organization? If the answer is "No," do not ask what Spike learned. It will take you on a tangent from which you may be unable to return.

Scenario B works. You need to get Shirley started right away. Ask a question which reflects your concern and need for an answer, and you will see results.

**Don't include the answer in your question.**

You do not have to put your answers in your questions. See if you can identify where the manager's conclusions are embedded in these questions:

- Isn't that your favorite movie?
- Don't you think Brian is the best worker?

In these two examples, you'll see that the manager's answer is contained in their question. That's a great movie. Brian is the best worker.

Your people should come up with their own conclusions. Empower your people. Help them think for themselves and come up with their own conclusions.  Don't include the answer in your questions.

---

**Be careful with the 'why' question.**

Think about the 'why' question.  What happens when you get a flurry of 'why, why, why' coming at you?  You get defensive.  When <u>you</u> ask a direct report a 'why' question, you can shut down and impede two-way communication.  That's not what you want them to do.

To be clear, asking 'why' has its place.  However, it should not be your first question, in most cases.  There are better questions for you to ask instead.

Here are some examples:
**Example:**  Why did you do that?
**Consider:**  What happened?

**Example:**  Why do you think that happened?
**Consider:**   What could you have done differently?

**Example:**  Why are you saying that?
**Consider:**  What is that about?

Try replacing 'why' with 'what' for just one day.  You will be amazed at how differently your people will respond.

**Understand how much you bring to the conversation.**

You do not have to be part of every equation. You may think: "I have experience and knowledge my people need to hear. It is important to share this every time I speak."

Don't get in the way of the question. Do you know how much you are 'in' every question you ask? We don't realize how often our own thoughts get caught up in the words we say.

**Examples:**
*Are you feeling as bad as look?*
*You look tired. What is wrong?*

Asking "What is wrong?" offers an opinion. It is more a statement than a question. What if nothing *is* wrong or they deny something is wrong? You might have created an opportunity for conflict with a poorly-worded question.

**Consider:**
*How are you doing today?*

This question opens up the conversation and allows the person to talk more freely.

**Example:**
*Tim, is Martha ever going to give you that report?*

This sounds accusatory. You are giving neither Tim nor Martha benefit of the doubt. Both of them could become defensive.

**Consider:**
*When can I expect the results from Martha, Tim?*
*Tim, what's the latest on the report Martha is working on?*

---

**Keep your questions simple.**

It sounds basic, but we often overcomplicate our communication. We tend to add words where we don't need to. We often drag out concepts to make things clearer to ourselves. We think out loud. Simple questions will get you the right answer.

There are three skills involved in creating a simple question. They have to do with:
- **Content**
- **Structure**
- **Meaning**

**Content:** Avoid business jargon, acronyms, initials or specialized language.

**Examples:**
- What is the NCOA for our next phase?
- Don't you think liquidity and marginalization is the key to this?
- Why such alacrity about this ROI number?

Avoid this kind of language. Know your audience. Abide by their need to understand, not your need to use 'big words.'

---

**Structure:** Consider the length of your question. If your question is too long, you will lose your listener.

**Examples:**
- Are you in a situation where you would value my input or are you in a place where the independent opportunity for thought is more beneficial?
- What part of the relationship between you and the team is the part that you consider to be the component that allows you to be as connected as you wanted to be in the last meeting?

**Consider:**
- Do you need anything from me?
- What is going on with the team?

---

**Meaning:** Simplicity creates effective communication. Don't ask something your people fundamentally can't answer.

**Example:** How are we going to restructure and fix this recurring problem?

**Consider:** What is one thing our department might start doing today?

---

To recap, these five fundamental guidelines to asking great questions will unleash your capability to be inquisitive.

1. **Don't ask a question unless you truly want an answer.**
2. **Don't include the answer in your question.**
3. **Be careful of the 'why' question.**
4. **Understand how much you bring to the conversation.**
5. **Keep your questions simple.**

Knowing the rules is one thing. Practicing and putting them to use is another. We have come up with a list of questions that will help you apply the five guidelines we have just revealed. Each one of these questions will be perfect at some time or another. Practice. Say these questions out loud. Use them, and see when each one is most effective for you.

1.  And?

2.  Because?

3.  Can you re-phrase that for me?

4.  Do you understand why I asked this question?

5.  Does your current way of dealing with things work for you?

6.  How does that play out day-to-day at work?

7.  How have you handled that in the past?

8.  How important is it to do something right now?

9.  How could you have handled that differently?

10. What are the consequences of following your instincts now?

11. What can you change about that situation?

12. What choice do you have?

13. What conclusions can you draw?

14. What do you need to focus on?

15. What does that look like?

16. What does that mean to you?

17. What else could you do?

18. What have you learned from this?

19. What matters to you?

20. Who do you know that is good at that?

So, our first coaching skill was **BEing a good listener**. We just covered **BEing inquisitive,** with guidelines that help you ask great questions. Let's move on, and talk about taking personal bias out of business: **BEing objective and centered.**

**Coaching Skills (3 of 3): BE objective and centered: Remove your filters.**

Stay calm. Know what's really going on. Strip away your own biases, so you can see everyone's point of view. That's being objective and centered. How can you do that? Remove your filters.

**We define filters as:**

**Experience, knowledge and values that influence how we think, listen, and communicate with others.**

When your filters are in place, you only interpret things as if you had said them. You don't search for what someone else means, based on their experience, knowledge and values. So, what are your filters?

- **Your personal agenda:** Self-contained directions and guidelines that you follow every day.
- **Pre-conceived notions:** Views you have held in the past, with or without adequate information and evidence.
- **Judgment:** Formal decisions you have already made in advance.
- **Experience:** Answers that worked in the past, based on what you have been through in your life.
- **Opinion:** Beliefs or thoughts you have on a variety of issues.
- **Values:** Things you hold most important as you relate to your job and working with others.

All these filters get in the way of being objective and centered as a coach. Your job is to realize how often your filters influence what you think, hear, and say.

To be an effective coach, you cannot let your filters get in the way of being objective and centered. All filters are different. Don't change your filters. Just BE aware of their role in a conversation.

---

**Filters can lead to assumptions.** Not everyone thinks the way you do. They have different experiences, different values, different opinions that influence the way they think, just as yours influence you.

Imagine a conversation in which no one keeps their filters in check. Everyone is led by their own biases, opinions and assumptions. People don't take time to understand each other. How much effective listening do you think will take place? How much effective communication will take place?

If we want to remove our filters, we have to understand them. There are two kinds of filters that affect the way we exchange messages with others. One has to do with words, and the other has to do with the meaning of the words. These two filters, words and meaning, can alter everything we think, hear and say.

You are in a business conversation, dealing with a problem. A direct report makes a statement. Your first filter, the Words Filter, might eliminate some of their words altogether. You don't believe them, perhaps, or you are really not interested. You lose words altogether. Your second filter, the Meaning Filter, works with the words that remain, and gives them a meaning that you can understand and accept. These filters delete parts of a message, change others, and add meaning that wasn't there in the original.

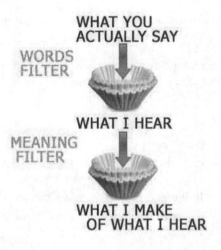

We start out with what someone said. The Words Filter plays its part. Then, we work with what we hear, and run that through the Meaning Filter. All we end up with is <u>what we make</u> out of <u>what we hear</u>. The original message is lost.

### DEVELOP YOUR COACHING SKILLS

- Can you identify your filters: agenda, experience, opinion, values, etc.?
- Do you know when your filters are in action?
- How do your filters influence your communication with others?

As a perceptive coach, you must notice body language, voice inflection and mannerisms. You must analyze the way your direct report chooses words, especially pivotal words such as 'feel' and 'think.' Pay close attention to all the messages a direct report sends you.

Can you see your direct reports' filters in action?
Can you identify ways to get past their filters and get to the truth?

**Stories from the Summit:**

*Eddie is a manager in a distribution center. He has twelve direct reports. One of his direct reports named Harry always has an excuse for not doing his job. Harry always uses the word 'but' when he feels defensive. Eddie interprets 'but' to mean: "I don't respect you, Eddie." This is Eddie's filter.*

*Whenever Eddie hears the word 'but' he gets very angry. Here's how it plays out:*

**Eddie:** *Harry, can you get these boxes on the truck in the next ten minutes?*

**Harry:** *Yes, Eddie, **but** I am swamped with the shipment that's over in aisle six. That has to be handled too, you know.*

**Eddie (getting upset):** *Harry, these boxes had to be out yesterday. They are late.*

**Harry:** *Yes, **but** it's hard to know what to do with the ones in aisle six too, you know.*

**Eddie (now angry because he heard '<u>but</u>' twice):** *Harry, get them moved, and get them moved now!!!*

*Harry throws down his clipboard and storms out of the warehouse.*

Eddie's filters played out here. Eddie can't stand the word 'but', because of strong negative associations he has to that word. He could have handled things with Harry more effectively if his filters were off. Instead, the situation escalated... and Harry walked off the job.

**Stories from the Summit:**

*Pamela Jean is an office manager for a small software company. Pamela Jean's love of animals is one of her most important values. It is also one of her filters. Pamela Jean's direct report, Maureen, comes to her with a problem. Here's how it plays out:*

**Maureen:** *I will have to leave early every day this week because Hershey, my sixteen year old dog, has an eye infection. I am worried about him.*

**Pamela Jean (overly sympathetic because of her filter):** *Oh, I can imagine. How much time do you need?*

**Maureen:** *I need to leave an hour early every day.*

**Pamela Jean (filter still on):** *Does that help you take good care of him?*

**Maureen:** *Oh, yes.*

**Pamela Jean:** *That's just fine, Maureen. I hope everything goes OK.*

*( Pamela Jean's next conversation)*

**Pamela Jean:** *Janice, can you stay and cover for Maureen? She has to leave early* *every day this week.*

***Janice:*** *I asked you if I could leave early today, because I have to meet my landlord. You didn't give me an answer.*

***Pamela Jean*** *(not as sympathetic for Janice because they don't share the same filter): You know this is a bad day for that. Can you do it tomorrow?*

Pamela Jean has her filters on. She can't see her favoritism to Maureen and the dog. Her filters are getting in the way of fairness to her direct reports.

**Don't let your filters get in the way. Identifying and understanding your filters helps you BE objective and centered.**

---

**Conclusion:**

Remember, there are three behaviors that will help you master the role of a coaching leader:

1. **BE a Good Listener**

2. **BE Inquisitive: Ask Great Questions**

3. **BE Objective and Centered: Remove Your Filters**

Develop these skills to be an effective coach. Work on them every day. Take each one individually: listening, asking questions, examining your filter. Decide what you want to practice each day. Examine what you need to do to be the best in that area.

Go back through this chapter in the weeks to come. Remind yourself of what you have to do, and practice until these qualities are a part of your everyday management style.

# Chapter Three
## Self-Discovery

Know yourself, and others will understand you. In your journey through self-discovery, you will find answers to these questions:

- What are my strengths?
- What are my weaknesses?
- What is my Why It Matters?
- How do I overcome my weaknesses?

This section could be the most challenging section of this book. You will take a good hard look at <u>who you are</u>. When was the last time you looked at <u>YOU</u>? With all the 'hustle and bustle' in your life, when did you last stop to examine yourself? Here's an opportunity to take some time out, time for yourself.

If the answers to these questions matter to you, this section is an important step on your way to the summit.

- Do you want to grow?
- Do you have room for improvement in any relationship in your life?
- Are you where you want to be in business? In your personal life?
- Are people seeing the very best of you?
- Are you living out your values?
- Are you happy?

All of us have values, personal motivations, and personal reasons for all we do. They affect everything we do, including the way we work with others and how we communicate.

It is important that you spend time getting to know you, all of you... what motivates you, what you value, what influences the things you do and say. The more you understand yourself, the more you will manage the way you communicate, lead, and work with others.

Self-discovery happens in three key areas. We use a diagram that helps you capture those three areas of your life. We call it the Discovery Shield, and you'll see it later in this chapter, once you are able to answer a few questions. The process will be simple, but it requires deep thought and time spent in reflection.

This chapter has three sections that examine:
- Your strengths
- Your weaknesses
- Your Why It Matters

Take the time you need in each section. It will be worth it. You will be taking steps towards positive change. It will be a change that leads to optimum performance and personal fulfillment.

We'll be asking you some questions. Invest the time you need and fill out your answers thoughtfully. The effort put forth will be worth it. Let's get started!

---

## Section One:  What are your strengths?

**Your strengths are what got you here.**  In this section, we'd like you to focus on your strengths at work.   What are three key strengths you put into practice consistently?

Pull out a blank sheet of paper to capture your thoughts. As you make your list, here are some questions to think about:

- What do you do well?
- What have people told you that you do well at work?
- Would others be able to identify your strengths?
- How do you know these are your strengths?
- What are the first three strengths that come to your mind?

### DEVELOP YOUR COACHING SKILLS

---

For most people, coming up with strengths is pretty straightforward.   For some however, it is a struggle.  It is hard to pinpoint, name it or call it something.  For others, this is hard because they simply don't know their strengths.  Consider asking others if you are at a loss.

Here are some examples of strengths that people have come up with:

- Work hard
- Team player
- Good decision maker
- Committed

- Highly energetic
- Love to learn
- Good communicator

Take all the time you need to determine what you really do well. Knowing your strengths and how to apply them at work is a vital first step in understanding who you are as a manager.

Take time to complete your list before you move on. Refer back to your 30 second commercial in the Introduction to help with this exercise. Please list your three strengths on a blank sheet of paper.

---

**Stories from the Summit:**

*Austin, CEO at a major retailer, was raving about his senior VP. "I love John," he said. "The man always gets things done the way I want, in a timely manner. The guy is just so reliable."*

*One day, Austin asked John: "Is there anything you would have me do differently, in terms of our working relationship?"*

*What John said struck a chord with Austin. "Ask me what some of my strengths are." Then he said: "Do you know I am very good at strategic planning?"*

---

Know your strengths, and share them.

Austin didn't take time to consider what John's strengths were, but John hadn't done anything to step out and showcase them, either.

When John knew his strengths and shared them, he deepened his relationship with his boss.

# Section Two:  Discovering Your Weaknesses

Your strengths have contributed to your past and present success. You will benefit from them as you develop in your career. But... your strengths will only take you so far.

**There will come a time when your weaknesses hold you back from reaching your personal summit.**

The first step to discovering a weakness is being able to call it what it is, a weakness! We all have them.  No one is exempt.  Yes, it's an 'area for improvement.'  But more importantly, it is a weakness. Let's call it that. It holds you back from being the best you can be.

We are talking about weaknesses in behavior, not skill.  Skills might include budgeting or making a great presentation. Behavior includes the way you listen, make decisions or communicate with others.  Any limits on behavior will drag down your relationships in the workplace and limit your ability to be an effective coach and manager.

---

**Stories from the Summit:**

*Joe is a very competent manager in product research.  His skills include organization, technical competency, and consumer expertise.  He is well respected in his industry, but his <u>behavior</u> isn't as highly developed as his <u>skills</u> are. That has become a weakness.*

*Joe is really boring. He's extremely detail oriented, which causes him to give people too much information.  Joe's emails average a page in length. In team discussions, it is difficult for him to get to the point.  He over-talks.*

*What happens?  Among peers and direct reports who like to get to the point or want less detail, Joe is perceived as someone who talks too much and can't focus. To others, he is perceived as overbearing.*

---

Offer Joe more education or better ways to be organized, and his communication skills will still be lacking. If he continues to disregard this weakness, people won't care how organized or technically competent he is, because his weaknesses are getting in his way.

Because of his behavioral weaknesses, Joe is an extremely organized and intelligent manager... who cannot connect with his people.

**Work on your weaknesses to reach your personal best, your personal summit.**

---

Here's how we define a weakness:

**Any behavior that negatively affects the way you lead, manage, communicate or work with others.**

Examine these questions. See if you can identify or relate any of them to your business behavior.

- Do you talk too much? Talk too fast?
- Are you afraid of confrontation?
- Are you intimidating?
- Do you micro-manage?
- Do you have problems making decisions?
- Do you avoid personal contact with important people?
- Do people clearly understand your directions?

Have any of those things ever held back your performance? Weaknesses in behavior can affect every relationship and every interaction you have, limiting your success.

## DEVELOP YOUR COACHING SKILLS

---

In order for you to work on improving your weaknesses, they have to be stated concretely and specifically.

**Consider this:** Is your weakness observable? If a weakness is not clearly observable or measurable, you can't do anything about it.

Subject your defined weaknesses to these questions and see if they hold up:
- Can you see it in action?
- Can you identify how often it happens, and when?
- How do you know this is truly a weakness?
- What have others said about your weakness?

39

**Do you need to clarify what your weaknesses really are?**

Sometimes, a weakness can be stated too broadly. Now that you have stated a weakness, simplify it, so you can actually work on it. Here are some examples:

| Vague statements of weakness: | True behavioral weaknesses: |
|---|---|
| I am not good at time management. | I am constantly overwhelmed, because I can't say "No" to new work. |
| I can be intimidating. | My body language is wrong. I cross my arms and talk too loudly. |
| I don't trust others. | I micro-manage everyone by checking every detail on every project. |
| I avoid confrontation. | I panic or shut down when confronted with an error I've made, or faced with a difference of opinion. |
| I judge people. | I do not listen, and I ignore input from people I don't like. |

Use these examples to see if your stated weakness is specific enough. You will understand our rationale when you start working on your weakness through a process we call Weakness Mountain.

Please list your three weaknesses on that sheet of paper, along with your strengths.

# Section Three: Why It Matters

Knowing your strengths and weaknesses is only the beginning. Before we show you how to get your weaknesses under control, let's look at just one more piece of the puzzle: what motivates you in your professional life. Everyone has an internal motivation. We like to call this motivation Why It Matters.

**Simply put, your Why It Matters is the real reason why you are who you are.**

When you focus on Why It Matters, your life will change. Take a moment to read this story:

---

**Stories from the Summit:**

*A manager wanted to see how his workers felt about their jobs. He went to his building site to take an informal poll. He approached the first worker and asked, "What are you doing?"*

*"What, are you blind?" the worker snapped. "I'm cutting these boulders with primitive tools, putting them together the way the boss tells me. I'm sweating under this blazing sun. It's back breaking work, and it's boring me to death."*

*The executive quickly backed off and went looking for another worker. "What are you doing?" he asked.*

*"I'm shaping these boulders into different forms, which are assembled according to the architect's plan. It's hard work, but I earn a good wage, and that supports my family. It's a job. It could be worse."*

*Somewhat encouraged, he went to a third worker. "What are you doing?" he asked.*

*"Why, can't you see?" beamed the worker, as he lifted his arms to the sky. "I'm building a cathedral! I can imagine the steps over there, filled with throngs of people here for a wedding. I can hear the bells ringing on Sunday morning. I can almost see the way the morning sun will shine through the stained glass. This is a great job."*

---

Three different people, all doing the same job, had three totally different ways of looking at their job: what they did, why they did it, and why the work matters.

The first worker focuses on *what he is doing*... breaking stones.

The second worker appreciates *why he's doing his job*... It's part of a plan. I make a living.

The third worker's focus on *why his job matters* influences everything he does: his work ethic, his attitude, and the way he relates to people. What is his Why It Matters? You might describe it as: "to see the big picture."

Everything we do comes down to personal motivation. We all have one, and everyone's is different. We are motivated by very different things, even if we are doing the same job.

## DEVELOP YOUR COACHING SKILLS

Along with your strengths and weaknesses, jot down five things that motivate you. When it comes to your job, what gets you going and keeps you moving? Capture those five things, and we'll review them in depth in a moment.

Your internal motivation, your Why It Matters, is the single most important factor that influences everything you do. It drives your behavior, it drives your communication, it drives how you get things done, and it drives how you relate to people.

---

**Stories from the Summit:**

*For as long as Sally can remember, she has been the person who keeps everyone happy. Sally hates conflict, especially people fighting or yelling at each other. Growing up, she was always the one that made sure everyone got along. Now an adult, Sally hasn't changed. She's still the one resolving conflicts, creating peace, and making sure everyone gets along.*

*Reflecting on her Why It Matters, Sally was able to determine that she has always been "the Peacemaker." Affirming her Why It Matters has given her clarity about why she does what she does. She knows why she likes and dislikes certain things about her work and her colleagues. She's aware of situations that motivate her and those that shut her down.*

---

Knowing your Why It Matters is going to bring you peace. It is going to help explain why you do things, why you enjoy things, and who you are.

**Why It Matters is your compass.**

Imagine a guiding force that you have used consistently, again and again, and continue to use today. You allow it to direct you, because it brings you success and happiness. It is the reason why you excel where you do, succeed in what you do, accomplish what you can.

One thing we can guarantee about your Why It Matters - it is hard to turn off.
In fact, it runs under its own power. It is what you do when you run on automatic pilot.

Anything that becomes over-used, even a good thing, will be abused. Your Why It Matters is no exception!

---

Let's look at Sally, our "Peacemaker." Sally is very effective at creating harmony, resolving conflicts, and making sure everyone is on the same page. Sally focuses on team unity and representation. Being a "Peacemaker" has helped her become a great listener, hearing all sides of every conversation. She always makes sure she is in a win-win situation.

What happens if Sally is *always* the peacemaker?

What happens when things aren't harmonious? How does Sally act? Does she back away? Run? Sally avoids taking risks that might affect team harmony. It is difficult for Sally to tell people what they need to hear. Sally does not like confrontation. As a manager, this creates havoc for Sally. She ends up with a unified team that has no clear direction, because they don't address problems.

**Manage your Why It Matters**

- Your Why It Matters, when abused, becomes a liability, not an asset.
- Your weaknesses are usually your Why It Matters allowed to run out of control.

Until you identify your Why It Matters and know when it is guiding your words and actions, you will lack direction. This affects everything in your life.

**Stories from the Summit:**

*Jan is President of a small retail bank. As the leader of her organization, she is a master at creating a strong team environment. Jan shelters her people from outside criticism and is personally committed to keeping everyone together, even through hard times. Jan's Why It Matters is "to protect."*

*When it works, Jan creates loyalty. Her staff loves her, because they know she will defend them. She is on their side. She has their best interests in mind.*

*When it doesn't work, when her Why It Matters should be turned off, Jan is over-protective. She becomes a micromanager. She takes on everything by herself. She doesn't allow her direct reports to grow. She also overlooks the weaknesses of senior staff if she believes the company is being protected.*

*Besides working herself to death, she's letting some of her people get away with things for which they should be held accountable. Jan needs to get her company under control. On the surface, things appear to be fine. Internally, however, people are suffering.*

**To live out your Why It Matters and use it to its fullest, manage it. Make sure it doesn't become a weakness.**

Figuring out your Why It Matters isn't merely important. It's vital to understanding who you are and what you do. Knowing what it is will help explain everything: your strengths, your weaknesses, and how to manage yourself.

To learn more about finding your Why It Matters, read '*Why It Matters: The Sherpa Guide to What You Are Looking For*', available at www.sherpacoaching.com/store.

44

Let's figure out your Why It Matters. We will end up with a short, simple phrase that explains your highest motivation in your business environment. To get you started, go back to your list of five things that get you motivated, and then answer the questions below. Take all of the time you need.

- What gets you going in the morning?
- What has always been on 'automatic pilot' for you?
- What are you determined to do, no matter what?
- Why is that so important to you?

Use the answers to these questions to come up with a single, clear statement of Why It Matters to you. Your Why It Matters has to be very personal and specific to you. It's not something as broad as, "making the world a better place" or "I want to make a difference." Those examples are too broad, not specific enough to your gifts and abilities and are the results of your Why It Matters. Here are some Why It Matters examples:

- To accomplish
- To earn praise
- To create agreement
- To be recognized
- To be valued
- To prove competency
- To be accepted
- To be a guiding light
- To serve

Now we are ready to put everything we have discovered in one place. The diagram that follows is called the Discovery Shield. Certified Sherpa Coaches use this in one-on-one coaching with executives across the world.

First, transfer your three strengths from that sheet of paper onto the 'strengths' section of the Discovery Shield. If you can refine your thoughts and better define your strengths, do that now.

Next, transfer those three weaknesses you listed, clarifying your thoughts as you go.

Finally, let's take that phrase you have arrived at: your Why It Matters and write it on the bottom half of the shield.

If you'd like some examples of what other people have done with their Discovery Shield, read on. But don't go too far until yours is complete, too.

---

# The Discovery Shield

STRENGTHS:

WEAKNESSES:

WHY IT MATTERS:

# Why It Matters: Examples

Here's what people have shared with us as they worked though their Discovery Shield. You can see how everything ties back to the Why It Matters: strengths and weaknesses alike.

| Why It Matters: To be needed | |
| --- | --- |
| Strengths | Weaknesses |
| • Loyal | • Emotional |
| • Compassionate | • Avoids confrontation |
| • Reliable | • Takes things personally |

| Why It Matters: To get things done | |
| --- | --- |
| Strengths | Weaknesses |
| • Completes tasks | • Impersonal |
| • Results oriented | • Intimidating |
| • Driven | • Pushy |

| Why It Matters: To be the expert | |
| --- | --- |
| Strengths | Weaknesses |
| • Detail oriented | • Can be too wordy |
| • Knowledgeable | • Do not listen well |
| • Technically sound | • Perceived as arrogant |

Discovering your Why It Matters will help explain why you do what you do, act the way you act, say the things you say. Understanding how to manage your motivations will help you manage your weaknesses. This releases the best of you, and lets you be who you should be.

## Section Four: Overcoming your Weaknesses

This takes us to our next step. Let's learn how you can tone down your weaknesses. Working on your weaknesses, perhaps completely overcoming them, helps you reach your personal summit and live out your Why It Matters. The time you invest in overcoming your weaknesses will be invaluable.

What has happened up to this point? You know what matters most. You know your strengths. You have identified your weaknesses. You know they keep you from reaching your personal best, your summit. So now what? It's time to work on them.

We created Weakness Mountain to help you get there. We want lasting change. Your journey to the summit must be more than a single step. It's not going to happen unless we break it down into manageable pieces.

Weakness Mountain will take you on a journey of acknowledgment and change. Here's how we take on a single weakness in business behavior, and deal with it:

- **Acknowledge:** Recognize and own your weakness.
- **Observe:** Notice and record your weakness in action.
- **Change:** Identify a replacement behavior for your weakness.
- **Evaluation:** Assess the effectiveness of your replacement behavior.

---

**Stories from the Summit:**

*Joan's Why It Matters is "getting things done."*

*Joan can't slow down at all, ever. She constantly accomplishes so much that she intimidates people. People avoid Joan, because they are afraid of her. When she delivers expectations Joan comes off as demanding. Her direct reports will not confront her or seek out clarity because they are afraid of being reprimanded.*

---

Specifically, Joan's acknowledged weakness plays out like this:
- She's demanding and curt when communicating with others.
- She does not engage people when giving them instructions.

We'll use Joan's example as we work through Weakness Mountain.

48

# Weakness Mountain:  A process for overcoming a weakness.

## Weakness Mountain
### Step 1: Acknowledge

The first step in this process is to acknowledge your weakness. You can't begin to improve if you refuse to be aware of a weakness.

To start, we'd like you to work on a single weakness that affects how you communicate. Push yourself to clearly identify a behavior that holds you back from communicating effectively.  We like to use a weakness in communication because it has the most direct effect on your own ability to live out your Why It Matters.

Pick one of the three items you listed on your Discovery Shield.

The weakness I am going to examine is:

_____

_____


## DEVELOP YOUR COACHING SKILLS

On a deep personal level, can you acknowledge this as a weakness?

Yes _____     No_____     Not yet_____

Does this weakness get in your way?
How do you know? Have other people told you?
Do you understand how it gets in the way of communication?

This is how I know for sure this is my weakness:

_____

_____


Describe it and how it plays out for you.  What happens to you when you exhibit this weakness?  How do you behave?

_____

_____

49

# Weakness Mountain
## Step 2: Observe

Being able to observe your weakness is important, so that you can understand the triggers that set off this behavior. You will need to watch yourself for a while. You'll be surprised how much more you notice when you get in the habit of observing and documenting your own behavior. Your memory is not enough. There is real power in observing and recording your weaknesses in real time, as you interact with others.

---

**Stories from the Summit:**

*Joan's assignment was simple: Every time she communicated with others, she was to observe how many times others spoke back to her. This was easy for her, because she had a meeting with a direct report almost every day. She used those meeting times to track the reaction she got.*

*What did Joan realize from her observations? She realized that no one spoke back to her, in meeting after meeting. She was shocked. Four of the five meetings were, as she termed it, 'a disaster' when it came to people responding to her. Through observation, she realized that she did not give anyone a chance to offer input. People were actually looking down when she spoke to them, as if they were being scolded. The conversation was very one sided.*

*Her observations:*
- *No one spoke back. The one time someone did, he said, "What?"*
- *No eye contact was made.*
- *Several people were wringing their hands, acting nervous.*

Observe the weakness you have chosen to study. Use these questions as guides:

- When does it happen most?
- Where? In what situations do you notice your weakness?
- Who? What? Does someone or something provoke it?
- How do I react? How is my body language?
- How often does it happen in a day?

Now, think about how you are going to measure and track your observations. What simple things can you do in order to observe yourself? Consider some of these ideas:

- Keep note cards with you and record each time your weakness exhibits itself, keeping in mind the questions above.
- Chart out the days of the week on a piece of paper and take a tally at the end of each day to see how many times your weakness showed up.
- Have someone you trust observe you in a meeting or conversation.
- Take notes in a meeting. Writing things down will give you revelations, much more so than just thinking about it.

This might be a good time to grab a bookmark, put it here, and put this book down for a few days. Track your weakness for a while.

Now what? Any revelations about this weakness?

- Do you have a better understanding of it?
- Do you need some more time to observe?
- Is it clear how your weakness gets in your way?

Do not be afraid to take the time you need to understand how your weakness plays out.

## Weakness Mountain
## Step 3: Change

We know change is hard. Sometimes, you know you have a weakness, you want to change, and yet you can't. It is much easier to stop doing something if you start doing something new in its place. We call this new thing a replacement behavior.

It's time to identify a replacement behavior for the weakness you are working on. We don't want you to come this far just to turn back.

You have to answer the paramount question: Do you want to live out your Why It Matters? Do you want to be your best? Is change worth it? Let your Why It Matters become the meaningful motive you constantly return to, as you work towards breaking your habit.

---

**Change requires commitment.** You must be willing and able to work on this. Commitment requires that you make a choice: Stop now, keep your current weakness, or replace it. It's up to you.

**Positive change always requires sacrifice**. A person who wants to lose weight probably has to give up a food they like. If you want to be self-employed, you'll need to sacrifice and save more aggressively. When things turn out better, the sacrifice is always worthwhile.

**It takes twenty-one days to change a habit, and this weakness is a habit**. In time, the weakness will fade, and new habits will form. It is going to hurt the first few times. Then you will be able to observe, be motivated as you see how well people react to a different approach and grow into a new way of being.

---

Stories From the Summit:

*Joan never wanted to run over people. She just wanted to make sure tasks were being completed on time. She became aware just how rampant "get things done" had become. Joan realized she really had to back off and change the way she was doing things.*

*Joan identified one replacement behavior to start: Ask a question for clarity and speak less by using no more than three sentences at a time. She decided to ask questions during her daily meetings and use three sentences in her weekly staff meetings. Both were measureable and obtainable for her. She was going to work on these specific action plans for the next month and summarize her findings.*

**Here's what Joan came up with as her replacement behavior:**

When I see that people have shut down and won't respond, I will execute these replacement behaviors:
- Change my body language.
- Take a deep breath.
- Ask a simple question.
- Give thanks for the answer.

## DEVELOP YOUR COACHING SKILLS

After you have observed your weakness, what can you start doing to replace it? We'd like you to take a minute to identify and write down something concrete, something different, that you can start doing tomorrow.

Keep it simple. Don't come up with an action plan that's too lofty, especially your first time around. We don't want you to go back to your old ways if you don't experience success right away.

Take the time you need here to write down a replacement behavior, or several, for your weakness. What replacement behavior is simple enough, yet dramatic enough to help you manage your weakness?

| My Weakness | My Replacement Behaviors |
|---|---|
| | |

## Weakness Mountain
## Step 4: Evaluation

In this final step, you will work with one replacement behavior and evaluate how successful it is. If it's not working, find a new one, and work with it for a while. Go back to the bottom of the mountain, re-identify the weakness if necessary, and observe once again. Then, you are ready for another replacement behavior.

It's important to have something to work on. Don't get overwhelmed. Revisit the replacement behavior in as much depth and as often as you desire. This keeps you on the path to your summit.

---

**Stories From the Summit:**

*When Joan first started asking questions and allowing people to talk, they were taken aback. They gave her blank stares and moments of silence, as if they did not know what to do. Joan wanted to jump right back to "getting things done," but she stayed with her replacement behavior, as hard as that was.*

*Eventually, Joan learned that her direct reports knew more than she had ever given them credit for. In time, she was "getting things done. "Joan did not have to constantly hover over people. They actually started coming to her and asking questions. With two-way communication, they were clear on what needed to be done. Joan was well on her way to changing the perception others had of her and effectively living out her Why It Matters.*

---

### DEVELOP YOUR COACHING SKILLS

Take your time as you evaluate whether your replacement behavior is working. Answer these questions:

- How have things been going?
- Is your replacement behavior working for you?
- How well are you handling the change?
- Is it better than the old way?
- Do you find yourself wanting to resort to old habits?

**Expect some relapses from your replacement behavior. This is normal.**

Give yourself an honest assessment.
- Is your replacement behavior too difficult? Too simple?
- Do you need to rewrite your replacement behavior?

Don't be afraid to adjust your replacement behavior if you need to. Don't give up. You are building new habits. When you succeed, reward yourself. Give yourself something that you need or want. Keep up the good work. Celebrate your victories.

Remember, simple changes often lead to big results. Don't lose sight of this. You do not have to reach the summit in a single step.

Achieve success by overcoming one weakness at a time. Once you have dealt successfully with one weakness, and found a replacement behavior that works, start working on the next weakness. You didn't get to where you are overnight. Don't expect to get to the new you overnight, either. Spend the time you need. Be patient.

Spend as much time as you need climbing through the process we call Weakness Mountain. Revisit it as often as you wish.

Because you live out your Why It Matters without thinking about it, you'll need to continually keep yourself in check. Getting rid of weaknesses is a prerequisite to progress. When you make a positive change by addressing a personal weakness, several things happen:

- You shore up good relationships and repair bad ones.
- The new respect you earn changes the way people see you as a leader.
- Most of all, you live out your Why It Matters.

# Chapter Four
## Setting Expectations: The Sherpa Way

A good manager's department runs perfectly, even when he's not there. In order to truly *be* as a manager, you can't do all the work. You have to be able to tell people, quite clearly, what needs to be done... and how you expect them to do it.

Have you ever gotten too deeply into details because one of your direct reports didn't get their work done properly? Perhaps they didn't understand what you wanted them to do in the first place?

Setting expectations means telling people exactly what needs to be done, in a way that helps them do the work.

Setting expectations also involves managing your weaknesses. In the last chapter, you learned how your weaknesses play out at work. Now we are going to talk about how your weaknesses affect the way in which you communicate.

**Every time you ask someone to do something, your weaknesses play a role.** How can that be? Let's look at some examples.

| Weakness | How your expectations play out |
|---|---|
| I talk too much. | People don't know what is important, or what they really need to listen to. You confuse your audience. |
| I'm afraid of confrontation. | You fail to say something important because you are afraid it might lead to an argument. |
| I can be overbearing, even intimidating. | People are afraid of you. They shut down before you ever ask them to do something. |

One of the most common forms of communication between a manager and a direct report will be the setting of expectations. Your weaknesses, if they are not managed effectively, can affect everything you do in a negative way.

Let's look at a detailed description of what an expectation is, and give you a simple process to create better communication between you and your direct reports.

**An expectation is an important task, goal, or project that requires a positive response from others to achieve it.**

Focus on two parts of this definition:

- **Positive response:** Have you ever delivered an expectation that was not well-received? We will teach you how to turn every expectation you deliver into something more positive... Making things good for your direct reports. Giving them something they want to do.

- **For others to achieve:** This is not yours to do! Have you ever stepped over your boundaries and completed tasks for others? Do people on your team do the same? How do things work out?

---

When managers don't know how to communicate what they want, they will choose to do work that others have been hired to do. They find it simpler and easier to do it themselves. Delegation disappears.

One of the most important skills a manager can develop is setting and communicating clear expectations. We'll give you a great process, but there's more to it than that. To get the desired results every time, you have to manage from a calm center.

---

**You are about to learn how to:**

- Avoid the pitfalls that lead to failure.
- Create an environment in which everyone wins.
- Get important tasks completed on time and under budget.
- Give your direct reports satisfaction and empowerment.

When you create clear expectations, you create opportunities for success for you and your team. Let's get started.

# Setting Expectations: The Sherpa Coaching Way

Don't throw out expectations randomly. Pick your battles and you'll know when to set expectations in a process-driven way. Here's how you will know when you need to apply this process:

**Set expectations when something's new, changed, urgent or broken.**

## NEW

Set expectations when dealing with something people have not seen before, or when an approach needs to be different than what you've done in the past. This applies to your work with individuals and with teams. 'New' can include new responsibilities, new staff, or new procedures.

*Here's an example:* Lori's department has been asked to take on the duties of payroll. Her staff is not familiar with payroll processing or their vendor's procedures. Lori must set new expectations for her staff so that they will be prepared for the new duties.

## CHANGED

This describes any situation, goal, environment, or circumstance that is different from the norm. This can mean a change in people or plans, a revised budget or new office space.

*Here's an example:* Craig is the manager of a call center. The bonus policy for his front line people now emphasizes completing more calls, at the expense of the old 'service at all costs' policy. This calls for training, measuring and monitoring ...all part of our process. A change in expectations must be communicated.

## URGENT

A task or a project has become pressing or even critical.

*Here's an example:* Donna is manager of the advertising division. She has to have the final draft of her new ad campaign delivered to her media consultants by Tuesday. It's Monday. Donna calls for a morning meeting to share expectations with her staff.

## BROKEN

We define 'broken' as anything that gets in the way of productivity and working relationships. Often, broken applies to poor results, performance, or behavior. Something is just not working.

*Here's an example:* Leon was charged with hiring twenty new consultants by the end of the month. The month has come and gone. Only nine people have been hired. Expectations have to be reset for Leon.

# Pre-Work for an Expectation

Before you climb any mountain, you'll spend time at base camp, getting ready. Setting expectations is that way, too. You'll need to do a little research and give your situation some thought before you start talking about it. We call this 'pre-work.'

Before you actually communicate an expectation, consider the details:
What needs to happen? Who are the best people for the job? What's my deadline?

Pre-work does not take a lot of time. Few of us, as managers, actually stop and reflect on what we are about to say to our direct reports. Why? We assume too much. We operate at lightning speed. We do not slow down to think. Make time to do this. Success does not happen by accident or come from momentum.

Pre-work allows you to complete your thoughts before you attempt to communicate a task to others. Pre-work can be summed up by these four questions:

- Is it realistic?                          • Is it consistent?
- Is it fair?                               • Can they do it?

Let's examine what you do in your preparation, and try to get a positive answer to those four questions.

**Is my expectation realistic?**
Is this a sensible, practical, and reasonable expectation for my direct report?
Does my direct report have enough resources and capacity to accomplish the desired outcome or result? If not, how can I help?

**Is my expectation fair?**
Is it impartial? Did I choose the right person for the task? Am I giving them too much? Think it through. Have we considered and balanced everyone's workload? Can we prioritize other work? When you've considered fairness, it improves your ability to communicate the expectation.

**Is my expectation consistent?**
Is this coming way out of left field? Does this align with the way we usually work? Are there special considerations? Are we establishing a new way of doing things that will continue? Does this create contradictions?

**Can they do it?**
This question can be the deal breaker. Do your people have the skills, willingness and availability to accomplish the task? Are we asking people to do things that they are fundamentally unable to do?

**Stories from the Summit:**

*Sterling is your top sales rep, a mover and shaker, good at creating opportunities and closing deals. Sterling can be spectacular at communicating the big picture and connecting with others. Details are not his strong suit, however.*

*Ask Sterling for a detailed report on month-to-date results and next quarter's projections, in a new Excel format. What happens? Usually, nothing. Is your request realistic? Can he do it? What do you need to do for him, so he can deliver the report you need?*

**Here's your pre-work:**
- Is this realistic?
- Is it fair?
- Is it consistent?
- Can they do it?

If you cannot answer these questions with a "yes," then you may need to adjust your expectations. Without pre-work, you can set everyone up for failure.

Let's change the way you set expectations, and see if you get better results. If you are working with a team, you'll use this process separately for each individual. Read on, and you'll find out why.

---

**Expectation Mountain**

Once we have considered our pre-work, we are ready to climb Expectation Mountain. Expectation Mountain is the Sherpa process for setting expectations.

There are four parts to the climb:
- Communicate
- Commitment
- Consequences
- Coaching

These are the four steps that make your expectations as a manager and coach become reality. As you gain practice using the process, teach it to others. It will set up a common language with your staff and peers.

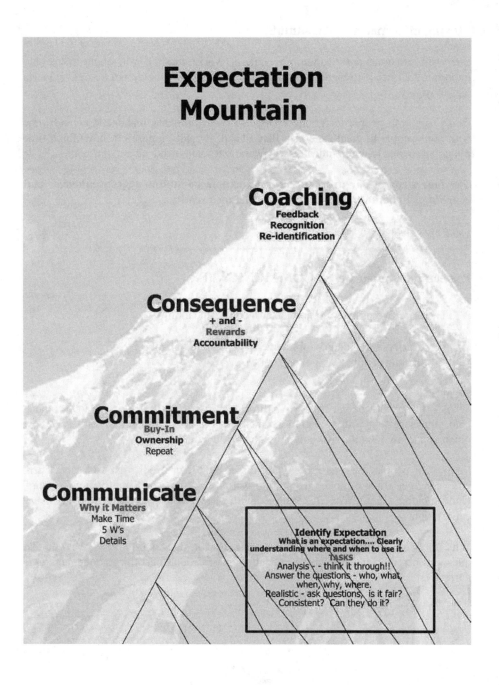

# Expectation Mountain

**Coaching**
**Feedback**
**Recognition**
**Re-identification**

**Consequence**
**+ and -**
**Rewards**
**Accountability**

**Commitment**
**Buy-In**
**Ownership**
Repeat

**Communicate**
**Why it Matters**
Make Time
5 W's
Details

**Identify Expectation**
**What is an expectation.... Clearly**
**understanding where and when to use it.**
TASKS
Analysis - think it through!!
Answer the questions - who, what,
when, why, where.
Realistic - ask questions, is it fair?
Consistent? Can they do it?

## Moving up Expectation Mountain

Ever had someone pass you in the hall at work, and tell you about something important that needs to be done right away? Expectations should not be delivered via 'drive by.'

Don't take your people for granted. Organize your thoughts, and spend enough time with your people to create success. Plan ahead. Prepare. Figure out how much time it's going to take to communicate an expectation. Then, make an appointment.

**The four steps in our process: communication, commitment, consequences and coaching will make your expectations become a reality.**

Let's look at each component in detail:

---

## Expectations, Step 1 of 4: COMMUNICATE

There are two primary components to communication.

- Clarify all the details, objectives, and desired outcomes.
- Include people's Why It Matters.

What is the benefit of knowing your direct report's Why It Matters? How could it help you in getting your expectations met? Think about it: People don't care how much you know... until they know how much you care.

Show your people you "get" them, you understand their needs, that you care. Then, you can get things done using motivation. Not your motivation. Theirs. Understanding their Why It Matters will change the way you deliver every expectation.

Why does this project, this task, this goal, matter in their world view? Answer that question correctly, and you have provided the motivation to get things done, and done correctly.

**Find out your employees' Why It Matters.** Ask them the following:
- Why do they work in this industry?
- Why do they wake up every day and go to work?
- Why did they choose *this* company?
- How do they define success?
- What motivates them?

With that in mind, clarify all the details, objectives, and desired outcomes you need to deliver. Now that you have communicated the expectation, you can move on.

## Expectations, Step 2 of 4: COMMITMENT

The key component to "commitment" is getting buy-in to the expectation you set. That comes when you master the language of leadership. The purpose of this step is to inspire mutual commitment. You may be eloquent in your delivery of expectations, but that doesn't guarantee that you've been effective.

What can happen if you do not have buy-in? Simply put, results fall short of expectations. Work output is not optimal. Employees go through the motions with a 'clocked out' mentality. Remember, we are trying to create success. Getting buy-in is a key step on the road to success.

What is commitment? Commitment is full engagement from both sides.

**How to promote commitment:**
Consider using some of these words with your direct reports:
- Give me the highlights of our discussion.
- What are your next steps?
- What is exciting about this?

Look for the message in their body language. Are they interested? Ask for comments with neutral phrases such as: "What do you think?" Then, stop for as long as it takes to get a response. Allow your direct report to express himself freely, with no repercussions.

**Do not move on without buy-in.** Be prepared to wait here as long as you need to. It is important that your expectations are clear, with full buy-in from your direct report before you move on. It ensures that each task is understood and will be completed.

DEVELOP YOUR COACHING SKILLS

List two ways you can ask a direct report to repeat information you have just given to them.

1._____

2._____

When you are sure you have their commitment, it's time to move to the next step.

## Expectations, Step 3 of 4:  CONSEQUENCES

Often, the word 'consequence' means a negative outcome or result.  This is not always the case.  Consequences can also be the rewards for a task well done.

Consequences can be positive, things like:
- Recognition for a successful team, or an individual's part in it.
- Team success. Many times, people have no idea how the things they do connect to the rest of the project. Tell them, and they'll give it their all.
- A simple "Thank you" can go a long way.  You will be surprised how a little more effort on your part can make a huge difference to your direct report.
- Show them that you know their Why It Matters.  Let your direct report know why the outcome is meaningful to them on a personal level, and why they are the right person to do the job.

*Be* sincere to *be* effective. Do not share a consequence, positive or negative, that you cannot deliver. Say what you are going to do, or don't say it at all.  Words matter. So does sincerity.

64

## Expectations, Step 4 of 4: COACHING

Coaching means to give feedback and check on progress. Offering feedback does not mean more work for a manager. Actually, it means less.

As a manager, you won't have to remember when to check back on every task, every project and every assignment. At the time you deliver an expectation, find a workable way to stay in touch. Make it work for you.

For example:
- Please email an update to me every Monday afternoon, covering…
- Let's schedule time right now, so we can sit down and review your progress.

**Do not count on people to come to you for feedback.**

Create check-in times in the beginning and you will know where a project is, all the time.

Setting and communicating expectations in a clear, consistent and concise way will change your life as a coaching manager. It also sets your relationship with your employees on solid ground.

### DEVELOP YOUR COACHING SKILLS

Let's see how well you can pick out the key components of Expectation Mountain.

Read through the script that follows. Find each of the 4 C's from the process. You may want to read the script four times, one for each step you're looking for. Circle where these take place:

- **Communication:**     Including Why It Matters
- **Commitment:**     Buy-in
- **Consequence:**     Rewards
- **Coaching:**     Follow up

## Expectations: The Lawn Leaper

*Ashburn: Terry, I have to tell you, you and your team are doing a great job on the Lawn Leaper. I just got some great news, too, an opportunity to showcase your project.*

*Cox: Thanks, Ash. What do you have in mind?*

*Ashburn: The CEO is coming in for some meetings, just ten weeks out. I don't want to pressure you, but... do you think we could show him some shiny new Lawn Leapers rolling off the production line while he's here?*

*Cox: I've got twelve people pushing pretty hard already. But, face time with the CEO is big, especially for the younger people on my team. I think it's fair to ask them, and see what they think.*

*Ashburn: I'd love to see this happen. But, no shortcuts, Terry. Everything is going so well. I'd like to make this a quality win, all the way to the finish line. Add some bonus money; we might move a few mountains, eh?*

*Cox: Well, I'm meeting with the team tomorrow morning, and I'll ask. If they make this idea their own, I think we could move the whole mountain range.*

*Ashburn: I'll keep this under wraps until you get back to me. This is a great opportunity for you and your team.*

*Cox: I'm really happy to have a chance, Ash.*

*Ashburn: I am going to help, any way I can. If there's anything we can take off your plate, keep you focused over the next ten weeks, let me know. See you tomorrow afternoon, 2 o'clock?*

## Key Components to Setting Expectations

- Apply the process to anything **new, changed, urgent or broken**.
- Do your pre-work.
- Know the 4 C's of Expectation Mountain.
    - o **Communicate**: Include their Why It Matters.
    - o **Commitment**: Get buy-in.
    - o **Consequences**: Do they know what to expect after they succeed?
    - o **Coaching**: Make sure you check in.

# Chapter Five
# Coaching Moments

Now, you have a way to get your expectations delivered. Using the Sherpa process, things will be done better, faster, with less stress. As a manager, you now have a new structure that helps you communicate and get commitment. But what about coaching? How do you truly coach people through an expectation, or any other time?

In this chapter, you will find answers to these questions:
- What are some coaching tools I can use?
- How will I know when to use them?
- How do I make time?
- What should I watch out for?

Let's continue our journey... from *doing* to *being*.

**Remember what a manager does:**
- Manage skills.
- Coach behavior.

**When dealing with direct reports, ask yourself:**
- Should I be managing or should I be coaching?
- Is this a behavior I'm dealing with... or an issue of skills?

When someone does not know how to perform a task, then you're seeing a lack of skill. Writing a report or filling out a form requires a skill. When people don't know how to do something, they need training. Training is part of doing.

Dealing with behavior is another thing. You aren't going to be a full time coach, so coaching your people won't be a lengthy process. We are going to do this one moment at a time, one opportunity at a time.

## Coaching Moments

Coaching moments are times when you should be coaching instead of training, consulting or managing.

**How do you know you are looking at a coaching moment?**
A direct report's behavior is not working. This behavior gets in the way of their productivity, or it hurts the way they work with another person or a team. When this happens, you have a 'coaching moment.'

**A coach draws out new behaviors in staff and colleagues.**
Coaching moments are those times when you help people change their behavior, rather than telling them what to do.

**We call them 'coaching moments' because they happen in an instant.**
You are walking down the hall to your office, or walking the floor of your manufacturing plant or hospital. People create a situation that is all about behavior. Coaching moments are immediate. They happen all the time.

---

Defined, coaching moments are:
**Impromptu, behavior-related situations in which coaching will produce better results than managing**.

---

**Here are two examples that may help you define your coaching moments:**

**Coaching moment #1:**

*One day Lisa comes into your office complaining about a fellow worker. "I can't stand her!" exclaims Lisa. "She just drives me nuts. Can't you do something about her?"*

Lisa needs to move from blame to acceptance. Her dislike of a fellow worker is not going to help anyone. Her behavior in front of you, right now, is wrong. You have to deal with it immediately. What do you say to Lisa? This is a coaching moment.

**Coaching moment #2:**

*Tina runs your credit department. She gives her staff weekly instructions that run way too long. People don't know what to focus on. Important things fall through the cracks. Tina comes in to your office and says, "No one is doing the work I asked them to do."*

You have a problem. Most likely, Tina is part of it. You'd like her to stop accusing others and contribute to a solution. It's your job to help Tina stop talking too much. As a coach, how do you help Tina out? This is a 'coaching moment.'

---

We are going to provide you with tools that will help you through these situations and other behavioral breakdowns.

*The Sherpa Guide*, our university text for executive coaches, has 30 tools for the coach. You won't need all of them. Based on our conversations with hundreds of managers in every working environment, we are going to give you the top four...tools that managers need the most.

---

**Learn these tools, how and when to use them, then practice, practice, practice.**

---

Your life as a manager will be changed dramatically. Why? Because people will stop their negative behavior, focus on resolving real issues, and do what they are supposed to do.

Practice using these tools until they become part of you. Put them in your coaching toolbox. Whenever you need them, you will find that taking them out and using them is so natural and effortless that you can *be...* instead of *doing*. Once the tools become who you are as a manager, you won't even have to think about them.

---

Remember, the title of this book is *'Be... Don't Do.'* To help you become a natural coach, we are going to give you three things to help you *be*, and three things you shouldn't do, as you learn to identify and master coaching moments.

You will remember that we gave you a similar list when we first introduced the concept of coaching. Reflect on these "BEs" and "DON'Ts" for coaching moments, and you'll be ready to pick up your coaching toolbox and try a few things.

---

**Here are three ways to BE... to find and master coaching moments...**

## BE observant.

Not every moment is a coaching moment. Know how to spot your coaching moments and take full advantage of them. Make the moment you are sharing with your direct report meaningful and useful to them. Don't waste time with situations that are trivial or beyond your control.

---

## BE calm.

You are at your best when you are relaxed and reflective. When you are in a coaching moment, take your time. Think through what you are going to say. Listen carefully. Help everyone stay centered. When you relax, they relax.

---

## BE confident. You will know what to say.

Coaching, the Sherpa way, might be a new concept. That's OK. Step out. Do it. Be confident. Whether you have been a manager for 20 years or 20 minutes, you know your job. Your bosses trust you to do your job. Trust that you will know what to say.

Here are three things you shouldn't do as a coaching manager:

## ... **DON'T** let the moment pass.

When you see a chance, take it. Learn by practicing. If you let an opportunity slip by, things will not get better. They'll get worse. If you step out and take advantage of a moment, things almost always get better. Be bold.

---

## ... **DON'T** talk just to talk.

You are in a coaching situation. Say enough so that you are understood. Then stop. More words won't make you more convincing. Convince by using just the right words, nothing more. Relax, and trust your coaching tools to do their job.

---

## ... **DON'T** let fear of confrontation get in your way.

Confrontation can be hard. It may seem easier to avoid a difficult conversation than to get into one. You can't change behavior without showing courage and confidence. When you have all the tools in place and know how to use them, confrontation will lead to the truth, not disagreement.

Now, let's start filling your toolbox with four new coaching tools. For each tool, we'll give you the exact words you need to say: Sherpa words.

---

We are about to share four coaching tools. These techniques will help you deal with the most common and troublesome business behaviors. Let's learn:

- **Separate the Person From the Issue**
- **QTIP**
- **Listen, Think, then Communicate**
- **The 3-Sentence Rule**

## Separate the Person from the Issue

Someone comes into your office, unhappy about the way things have turned out. They are ranting and raving. They need your attention and they need it NOW.

When your direct report is upset, it's usually about people. Managers get involved with 'people problems' because a direct report doesn't want to change their attitude or handle a situation on their own.

| Use When: | Sherpa Words: |
|---|---|
| People go after each other. | What is the issue here? |
| Blame is in the air. | Can you think of the issue and not the person? |
| People are emotional. | How do you take personality out of the equation? |

Talking about what your direct report is 'feeling' is not going to get you very far. Emotions add to problems. When someone brings you their negative emotions, and especially when they are visibly upset, it is easier, or maybe it seems more sympathetic to ask: "What is wrong? Tell me what happened."

Feelings do not solve problems.

What if you asked a different question: "What is the issue here?"

The issue should always be the center of a business discussion, not personality. People can argue for so long that they forget what their original problem was. As a coach, your role is to help direct reports deal with issues.

**A flip chart is a very good way to create focus.**

**Stories from the Summit:**

*Eric is a manager in a global cosmetics business. He has 30 direct reports. When Eric's team 'butts heads', he has to get past their feelings and get to the root of the problem.*

*One of his biggest coaching tools has been a flip chart. In Eric's office, the flip chart moves the focus away from personalities to a shared experience: defining the problem. His working environment has totally changed just because of that flip chart.*

**<u>Separate the Person from the Issue:</u>  How to use this tool**

Here's how Eric used the Flip Chart

*Eric:  What is going on in the field? How are the reps doing?*

*Terri:  I have no idea. I can't get out on the road.  Lisa is always annoying me with her petty questions.*

*Eric:  What will it take for you to get out and see some people?*

*Terri:  Lisa.  Gone from my life.*

*Eric:  What is the issue, Terri?  (using his flip chart)   Let's discuss what you need to handle here, and still get out to see our sales reps. Can you list three things?*

*Terri:  Well, Lisa needs more training so I don't have to do her work all the time.*

*Eric:  (writes the word 'training' on the flip chart) Let's look at the training she's going to need, and make it happen.  What else?*

*Terri:  I need to schedule a time every week to get out. It's got to be a permanent time slot, so everyone knows what to expect.*

*Eric:  Perfect, Terri. That's two. (writes the words, 'in the field').  Give me one more.*

*Terri:  I could spend three or four hours a week doing some quality control with Lisa so she knows she's doing things right.  I guess I really haven't spent enough time to help her get comfortable.*

*Eric:  Good. (writing 'extra time with Lisa')We have three things to work on. Let's see if we can get this all done by the end of the month.  Let me know next week how you are doing with these three items.*

## DEVELOP YOUR COACHING SKILLS

- How will you use the flip chart as a coaching tool?
- Give an example of a scenario in which you could use this tool right now.
- Refer to the guidelines and work through that scenario. What will you say?

## QTIP

When things are taken personally, what happens? People say things they regret. People end up angry and frustrated. Ultimately, people and performance both get hurt. When things are taken personally, people react much more than they reason. They don't look at the issue; instead they focus on feelings.

| Use When: | Sherpa Words: |
|---|---|
| People share negative emotions. | What is this really about? |
| Emotions hurt someone's ability to work with others. | How else can you look at this? |
|  | What is the real issue? |
| People take things personally. | What and who can you control? |

The QTIP tool goes right along with 'Separating the Person from the Issue'. This tool helps you get past emotions, and back to business.

## The letters in QTIP stand for Quit Taking It Personally.

When people take things personally, it hurts communication and it hurts performance. Do you know anyone in your work environment who takes things personally? Is there someone working for you right now who thinks everything is personal?

You might want to consider presenting him with a QTIP. We use a simple cotton swab to serve as a touchstone, a reminder that taking things personally is not an acceptable business behavior.

Of course, walking up to someone and handing them a QTIP won't solve the problem, will it? You will have to explain what it means, and have a meaningful conversation.

Once you have had that conversation, the QTIP is an effective reminder any time your direct report starts taking things personally. They can carry one in their pocket, reach in and touch it. You can hand them another one when the need arises, or you can simply say 'QTIP' softly, to remind them: quit taking it personally.

**<u>QTIP</u>:  How to use this tool**

**Stories From the Summit:**

*Mamie works in hospitality. She is emotional, to say the least.  She thinks with her feelings on every level.  Right now, Mamie is blowing up over some perceived insult.*

*Her manager needs to have that conversation we talked about, and starts by saying: "Mamie, I really don't care about your feelings."*

*Mamie sits back in her chair in disbelief.*

*Her manager continues: "I care about you, but I <u>do</u> <u>not</u> care about your feelings. Your feelings are related to things that happened a long time ago, or last weekend.  Your feelings are not based on what you <u>think </u>about this issue."*

*"I have something for you. (gives her the Q-tip)  Mamie, do you know what QTIP stands for? It stands for <u>Q</u>uit <u>T</u>aking <u>I</u>t <u>P</u>ersonally."*

*Mamie pauses and laughs.*

*Manager:  "This is not about your feelings.  I want to know what you are thinking. That's the only thing that's going to help me out.  What is the issue?"*

## DEVELOP YOUR COACHING SKILLS

QTIP can also be used for an entire team. Consider using it in your next staff meeting:
- Pass out the Q-tips.
- Ask them what a QTIP means to them.
- Write responses on flip chart.
- Tell them what it stands for and discuss.
- Use it for team building.

## Listen, Think, then Communicate

Our next tool, 'Listen, Think, then Communicate' is designed for people who need to engage in active listening. Remember our definition from early on: Listening is the *conscious effort to hear.*

When you catch a direct report trying to defend himself, time after time, share 'Listen, Think, then Communicate' with him. It's a three-step process that reminds your direct report to control what he says and to respectfully engage others.

| Use When: | Sherpa Words: |
|---|---|
| People talk too much. People jump to conclusions and assumptions. People speak without thinking. | Sounds like it didn't work too well. What could you have done differently? Are you sure you heard them correctly? Are you sure they understood you? |

**Here's the process to share with your direct report:**

# Listen: Listening is defined as "the conscious effort to hear." Listening is a skill. Listening takes practice. Listening takes effort.

To really hear what people say to you, listen to their words. Give them your full attention. Connect with them. Look at their body language. Listen to their tone of voice.

# Think: Thinking is judgment. Your natural tendency is to respond to what people say, right away. Don't. Take time to think through what this person is trying to say. Remember, if you are consciously hearing, you won't plan your response while someone else is still talking. Give yourself time to process what you are hearing.

Have you ever thought to yourself: "That didn't come out right? I should not have said that. I put way too much emotion behind those words." We all have. Once words leave your mouth, you can't take them back. You can apologize. You can offer further explanation, but you can't take words back.

Thinking allows you to communicate with confidence and purpose. Make sure this becomes a habit.

**Communicate:** Communication is everyone's responsibility. Don't expect that the person you're talking to will pay the same amount of attention as you do. No matter what they do, you need to hold up your end of a business conversation.

First, clarify that what you heard is what they meant. Then, deliver a clear and well-reasoned response. Repeat as needed for clarity.

---

### Listen, Think, then Communicate:  How to use this tool

**Stories From the Summit:**

*Leana is an associate at a paper converter.  She tends to say exactly what she thinks.  Leana has gotten herself into trouble by telling colleagues that they are not doing the job as well as she is.  She won't listen to anyone's explanations or pitch in when they have a problem.*

*Leana knows her relationship with her peers is NOT working.  She wants to do something about it.  People tell her she doesn't listen.*

*Leana's manager has to deal with Leana's behavior.  She decides to share 'Listen, Think, then Communicate.'  Leana's manager uses the following grid to help Leana understand and apply the concept.*

Leana's manager offers this: "Let's work down the left hand side of this chart, Leana. It says: "What do you have to do in order to be successful in these areas?"

| **What** do you have to do in order to: | **How** are you going to do it: |
|---|---|
| Listen: | Listen: |
| Think: | Think: |
| Communicate: | Communicate: |

- Listen: What do you have to do to listen more effectively?
- Think: What do you have to *think* about while you are listening?
- Communicate: What do you have to remember when you are *communicating*?

Leana answers these questions.

Then Leana's manager goes down the right hand side of the chart and asks: "How are you going accomplish this?"

- "How do you arrive at a fresh, new *listening* ability? "
- "How do you create a *thinking* atmosphere for yourself?"
- "How are you going to be an effective *communicator*?"

The focus is on the chart. Everything is objective. Leana decides *what* she has to do. Then, she walks through the chart a second time, and decides *how* she is going to do these things. Because she's talked it through with her manger, she has made a commitment, and has an accountability partner.

## DEVELOP YOUR COACHING SKILLS

Can you identify someone on your staff that might need this tool?

- Someone who says things and later regrets it.
- Someone who jump to conclusions without all the information.
- Someone who needs to slow down before they talk.

Practice. Know when and how to use 'Listen, Think, then Communicate'. Look for opportunities, and take advantage of them.

## The 3- Sentence Rule

Often, people who talk too much or too little just don't know what else to do. This tool, the 3-Sentence Rule, offers them another way to handle their communication.

When anyone delivers a message, involving people is important. It seems simple, but it's hard for people who go into too much detail, or those who like to hear themselves talk. People have to be taught to stop and think about how they are communicating, or they'll never change. This coaching tool helps people to do exactly that:

| Use When: | Sherpa Words: |
|---|---|
| People talk too much. | Can you re-phrase that in three sentences? |
| People don't engage others when communicating. | Do you need to use all those words? |
| People have trouble communicating their thoughts. | Can you give me the main point of what you just said? |

**The '3-Sentence Rule' is a framework that allows people to:**

- Slow down.
- Think about what they want to say.
- Package it in a way that makes sense and engages others.

When you have to address the business behavior of someone who talks too much, you will teach them the '3-Sentence Rule,' and give them a chance to practice with you.

Simply stated, this tool helps your direct report to speak more succinctly, three sentences at a time. So how do you structure those three sentences?

The first sentence in the sequence is the **introduction**: the big-picture idea.
The second sentence is the **theme**: the specifics you'd like to get across.
The third sentence is a **question**.

Here is an example:

*"I have a new dog at home.*
*I'm taking him to obedience training tonight.*
*Is it a problem if I leave a few minutes early?"*

**3-Sentence Rule: How to use this tool**

**1) 1st sentence:** INTRODUCTION. Grab your audience. Make sure they know that what you are about to say is important. This is called the 'effective introduction.'

> *"I think this project will make you more valuable to the company."*
> *"I'd like your opinion on something important."*

**2) 2nd sentence:** THEME. State the goal. Validate what you just said with some data, facts, or important information. Make it simple and straightforward.

> *"We are looking to revamp customer service, with you in the lead."*
> *"By learning this design process, you'll add value to everything you do."*

**3) 3rd sentence:** Ask a QUESTION, and then stop. Wait as long as you have to for a response. Asking a question immediately engages the listener.

> *"How do you see us proceeding?"*
> *"What do you think?"*

Stay there until you have a response from the person you are communicating with.

### DEVELOP YOUR COACHING SKILLS

---

The reality is, almost everyone can benefit from using this technique. How can you use this concept yourself? Would it help you communicate more effectively? Try it in your next meeting or one-on-one, and note the results.

---

**That covers our four coaching tools:**
- **Separate the Person From the Issue**
- **QTIP**
- **Listen Think, Communicate**
- **The 3-Sentence Rule**

Pick one of the four tools. Start to use it. Master it. Make it a habit. Then, do the same with the next coaching tool, until all of them come into play naturally.

We have asked you to become a coaching leader.

Let's create an action plan, so you can *be* all of that.

## Chapter Six: Accountability

Accountability is a process that ensures that activities within a system may be traced uniquely. Accountability involves making, keeping, managing agreements and expectations.

# Accountability measures Impact On Business

Responsibility is doing the job itself. Accountability is making sure the job gets done. It's important to understand and agree about who is responsible for what, and who is accountable for the end result.

Individual accountability is a willingness to answer for choices, actions, and behaviors. You and everyone else around you should take ownership of the right things, and nothing more.

Personal accountability means taking ownership of what belongs to you, and then applying the best of your skills and the best of your behavior.

# Things to know about accountability

- Accountability means you are the one who will take credit or blame.

- You can't delegate accountability. Know who you should delegate responsibilities to and the best way to delegate to these people.

- Someone gives you a job to do. You can get someone else to do it, but you are still accountable for the results. If the job isn't done right, the only person to blame is you, because even though you've delegated it, you are still accountable.

- If you work for a boss, be clear about what you will be held accountable for. If you are not clear, you would do well to find out.

- Accountability is directly related to integrity. For better or worse, can you say "I did that. That's my best work."? Integrity is being consistent in doing the right thing in all aspects pertaining to your work.

- Following standards and creating an atmosphere of stability helps you be a role model for your direct reports in paying attention to accountability.

# Accountability Defined

Accountability ensures that activities within a system may be traced uniquely.

Let's break this definition down:

"Ensures that | **activities** | **within a system** | **may be traced uniquely**."

- **Activities**: the job you do, the things listed in your job description.
- **Within a system**: your unit, section, department or floor.
- **May be traced uniquely:** "The buck stops here". There is ONE person accountable for the results of a job, program, project, or event.

We represent the facets of accountability by a comparison to your house. We call it Accountability House. Let's visit each room in the Accountability House.

# Accountability House: The Kitchen

Think about the kitchen: you spend a lot of time there. Think about the personal nature of the kitchen. If someone walks into your home and starts to rummage through your kitchen drawers, what is your reaction?

Needless to say, that is unusual behavior. People do step into each other's territory, their roles and their responsibilities. The kitchen serves as an analogy for what are we accountable for. Think of your job description as your kitchen.

## What am I accountable for?

Using the form on the next page, make the following entries:

First column: List significant tasks involved in your job. Items found on your job description such as staff development, project management, etc.

In the second column, rate the importance of the task to the organization and your department, on a scale of 1-5. '1' means low, '5' means high. Importance is about Impact on Business.

The third column, the 'x' indicates you will multiply two numbers

In the fourth column, rate your personal enthusiasm (passion) for the task. Do you like to do it? Rate using on the same 1-5 scale.

When deciding on a number, think about these questions:
- How much do I care about this?
- How well do I perform on this task?
- What would people say about how I do this?
- How comfortable am I about doing this?

In the final column, we multiply the Importance rating by the Passion rating, to produce what we call the I P factor: Importance times Passion. This exercise helps you assign a numerical value to the importance and passion of what you do every day. The I P factor produces a value that reflects both the value of each task and the likelihood you'll be able to work it through to completion.

# WHAT am I accountable for?

| WHAT am I accountable for? | Importance 1 to 5 | Multiplier | Passion 1 to 5 | Product/ Priority |
|---|---|---|---|---|
| | | X | | |
| | | X | | |
| | | X | | |
| | | X | | |
| | | X | | |
| | | X | | |

Remember, 1 is a low score, 5 is the highest.

High numbers, up to the highest possible score of 25, indicate a good chance of success. High importance, high passion. When importance is high and passion is low, a problem might be indicated. Any score under 15 is a task that should be examined. What else could you do? How else could you get the job done? Could someone else do it? Could you use resources, training to be more successful?

# Key Questions
## What are you accountable for?

How well are you managing your time as you do what you are required to do?

_____

_____

Are there any items that could safely be added to or removed from your list?

_____

_____

Looking at the item with the lowest score, what ONE thing could you start to do differently in order to be more accountable and more effective?

_____

_____

As you have worked through this exercise, what's your biggest 'take-away' about what you are accountable for?

_____

_____

# Accountability House: **Dining Room**

Who am I accountable to?
Who am I accountable for?

Think about the dining room: It is where you have your meals. It is where your family and friends gather. It is the room where the people are. Similarly, this Accountability Dining Room represents the people in your work life, sharing your table.

Here, we will repeat our earlier exercise, thinking about the people you work with. This is a private exercise and for your eyes only.

In the first column, the 'Who' column, write down significant people's names.

In the second column, rate the importance of the person to the organization and your department, on a scale of 1-5. '1' means low, '5' means high. Importance is about Impact on Business.

In the third column, the 'x' indicates you will multiply your two numbers.

In the fourth column, rate your personal enthusiasm (passion) for this individual. Do you like them? Do you enjoy this person's company? Are you passionate about them, and about their contributions?

When deciding on a number, think about these questions;
- How much do I care about this person?
- What would they say about me?
- Do we like each other?
- How comfortable am working with this person?

In the final column, we multiple the Importance rating by the Passion rating, to produce what we call the IP factor.

# WHO am I accountable TO?

| WHO am I accountable TO? | Importance 1 to 5 | Multiplier | Passion 1 to 5 | Product/ Priority |
|---|---|:---:|---|---|
| | | X | | |
| | | X | | |
| | | X | | |
| | | X | | |
| | | X | | |
| | | X | | |

Remember, 1 is a low score, 5 is the highest.

High scores, up to 25, are good. High importance, high passion.

Look at low scores, especially cases in which the importance and passion scores are different from each other.

# WHO am I accountable FOR?

| WHO am I accountable FOR? | Importance 1 to 5 | Multiplier | Passion 1 to 5 | Product/ Priority |
|---|---|---|---|---|
| | | X | | |
| | | X | | |
| | | X | | |
| | | X | | |
| | | X | | |
| | | X | | |

Remember, 1 is a low score, 5 is the highest. As before, look at cases in which the importance and passion scores are different from each other.

# Key Questions
## Who am I accountable for?

How are you allocating your time with your key people?
(Too much, Too little, Just right)

_____

How well are you doing at holding people accountable for their responsibilities?
(Very well, Average, Poorly)

_____

How well are you doing at being accountable to those you report to?
(Very well, Average, Poorly)

_____

Who is difficult for you to supervise?  What makes it difficult for you?

_____

_____

What's your biggest takeaway around who you are accountable "to" and "for"?

_____

_____

# Accountability House: The Living Room

What's stopping you from being accountable? Think about the living room: This is where the secrets are shared. This is where you sit down and figure out what is really going on. Here, in Accountability House, you find out what is preventing someone from being accountable.

These four concepts explain why people are not accountable for the work they have to do:

## The Comfort Zone

Accountability issues arise with people who are comfortable exactly where they are, and thus resist change. Understanding how closely your direct report stays in their comfort zone allows you to help them improve.

The comfort zone can mean different things to different people. A direct report who appears adventurous may not be as brave as they seem. They may take on new projects, unique challenges, all the time. That's because they are confident in their current skill set. Ask them to do something that requires learning new skills, and they could go into 'panic mode'. People don't like taking ownership of things they don't know much about.

The best way to see whether your direct report is stuck in a comfort zone is to draw the following picture for them, discussing each zone starting from the center comfort zone:

### In the center: The Comfort Zone
Where we like to stay. We know it. We like it. It's non-threatening.

### The next area: The Learning Zone
A place where you are in control, but learning something new. Good examples would be a craft class or a dance class: something new you choose to do, because you are excited about the results.

### The outer circle: The Panic Zone
It's a place where you are terrified. You are uncomfortable, because you are not in control. For some people it's confrontation, for others it is a cocktail party. Your panic zone is the place where fear overcomes your ability to do anything.

# Life begins at the end of your Comfort Zone

Do you ever:

Concentrate on the parts of your job you know and like, to the exclusion of other things, such as making sales calls or filling out paper work?

Procrastinate? Do you put things off or avoid doing them because they are outside your Comfort Zone?

What are your comfort zones? Do they prevent you from being accountable?

_____

_____

_____

_____

_____

# Accountability House: True Outcomes

'True outcome' is defined as your own personal truth. This is based on your ability to shape reality to your own purposes. The end result, your perceived reality, is often arrived at through avoidance or denial. Sometimes, we see things as okay, acceptable, even though we know they are really not that way.

## Case Study #1:

A manufacturer of fork lift equipment designed a revolutionary new braking system, which requires no maintenance. Unfortunately, some of the free-floating components in the braking system shifted as the vehicle moved through its final tests, making an odd squeaking noise. Everyone was so enthralled with the revolutionary design concept that no one wanted to mention how the brakes squeaked. They went through the entire testing process, without anyone wanting to admit they had a problem. This new equipment went into manufacturing and production, and was delivered to customers with the squeaking noise in place, right along with the new technology. Ultimately, customers were not afraid to complain about the noise the machine made, despite the revolutionary technology. As a result, the product was unacceptable, and had to be redesigned and reworked at a tremendous cost.

## Case Study #2:

Mary was a bank teller. She told her manager she deserved a raise. She had worked there longer than some of her colleagues and was much more prompt. Her manager consistently and repeatedly told her it was not possible.
She decided to take money from her till, so she would have the money she deserved.
She was caught on a security camera. Needless to say, she was fired.
She said: "You didn't want to give me a raise so I had to take it into my own hands and deal with it." Her own true outcome did not line up with reality.

## *Your* truth is not always *the* truth.

Can you think of a time when true outcomes prevented you from being accountable?

_____

_____

_____

# Accountability House: Fear

The next reason we are not accountable is fear. What role does fear play in accountability? Fear is a basic emotion that can be hidden, yet it is constantly present in the work environment. Fear is a driver that few people allow themselves to think about. Fear prevents us from doing things we know we must do. As soon as you can talk openly about fear, and describe what people are afraid of, you will have an easier time solving accountability issues.

There are so many fears that we experience, here are the top ones we encounter.
- Fear of looking foolish or incompetent.
- Fear of conflict and confrontation.
- Fear of failure.
- Fear of success.
- Fear of the time and effort needed.
- Fear of being called 'on the carpet'.
- Fear of appearing as an outsider.
- Fear of the future.
- Fear of creating chaos.

Fear is dealt with by addressing it. If you discuss it honestly with your people, then you can discuss ways to deal with it. The best way to deal with fear is looking at it straight in the face.

Acknowledge it and call it what it is. It is called fear.

> "The enemy is fear. We think it is hate, but it is fear."
> -Mahatma Gandhi

Can you think of fears that have prevented you from being accountable?

_____

_____

_____

# Accountability House: Blame

The final issue in the Living Room of Accountability is blame, another big stumbling block for many leaders. When you blame, you stop being accountable for what you have to do. Blame is a funny game. Pointing the finger at someone else can be one of the biggest ways to avoid being held accountable. If you blame, you think the problem might go away. If you blame, you think people might not ask you again. If you blame, you think, you look good and someone else looks bad. None of this is true.

Why is it so easy to blame? Well, it can save someone the effort of being caught up in an issue they never cared about, don't want to be involved in and don't have the energy for. If you play the game of placing blame, you welcome negative consequences.

If one of your direct reports is placing blame, using it as an excuse, as a way to avoid being accountable, speak directly to them. Say this: "You cannot bring anyone else into this discussion. This is just you and me". This can be effective if you are dealing with issues such as:

1.    Personal phone calls
2.    Personal internet use
3.    Gossiping
4.    Socializing
5.    Extended lunch/breaks

# When you blame others, you give up your power to grow.

Placing blame: Can you think of times when this has happened?

_____

_____

_____

# Chapter Seven
## Make Coaching Skills Stick

This is it. It's time for a decision. Will you close this book and go back to your day-to-day routine, or will you change the way you work with people?

Will you continue to do things, and do more things, or will you try to *be* instead, and find out who you really are?

Are you happy with your current state of affairs as a manager? Is everything working perfectly for you, all the time? If so, close this book. You are done. Thank you for reading.

If you have room to improve, then stay with us a little longer. It's going to be worth it. We want to help you create lasting changes. Here are some questions we will need answers for:

- How might coaching affect me and the people around me?
- Who can help support me on my coaching journey?
- How do I make sure I don't lose what I have learned in this book?

You know what a coach is, and what a coach does. You can recognize coaching moments and you have tools that get results. This doesn't happen because this book passed through your hands. Coaching is like any other talent. You must practice to see great results. We want you to *be* effective... and <u>stay</u> effective.

This chapter will help you establish an action plan using a follow-through procedure.

---

**Let's start by creating your Action Plan:**

The Action Plan serves as a contract. Promise yourself you will start using and continue to use what you have learned here. Your action plan will be a single sentence using action verbs. Without *action*, there is no movement.

If you really want coaching to be a part of you, make a promise, and keep it. Make a commitment to work, practice and live the concepts you have learned.

**Read through and answer these questions:**
- What really struck you about this book, and the Sherpa concept?
- Are you going to work on your listening skills?
- What do you want to get better at? The 3-Sentence Rule? Expectations?
- Do you understand your own Why It Matters and how it plays out?

We have covered a lot of material. Review the Table of Contents, and key areas in each chapter. Find things you would like to continue working on. Whatever you want to be good at, discipline and practice will make it a reality.

# QUESTION

This activity helps you follow your action plan to successful conclusion. It's called QUESTION. Each letter in the word 'QUESTION' is a step in the process, designed to help you follow and execute your action plan.

We'll use a worksheet to capture each step. Make a copy, if you'd like, so you can do this several times. There are some tips on the following pages.

| | |
|---|---|
| Action Plan<br>Write it out in DETAIL: | |
| **Q** - Have you asked enough **questions**? | |
| **U** – Do you **understand** it? | |
| **E** – When to **evaluate**? (a series of dates) | |
| **S** – Is it **specific** enough? | |
| **T** – **Trick**, do you have one? | |
| **I** – Is it **important** and positive? | |
| **O** – Do you **own** it? | |
| **N** – **Name** an accountability partner. | |

## Writing down your Action Plan

Here is how to use the QUESTION process:

The first row is your action plan. This is written in one sentence. It should be clear and easy to understand. No one else has to understand it the way you do. Memorize it. Think about how you will live it out, day by day.

**Here are some examples from managers we have worked with:**

- Use the '3-Sentence Rule' at my weekly staff meetings.
- Show I am listening to my boss, by leaning in slightly when she talks.
- Use questions to help Lorie solve the problems she brings me.
- Get up and move away from my desk when direct reports are in my office.
- Walk through the office every day, stopping three times for conversation.
- Practice 'Listen, Think, then Communicate' with Terri.
- Teach 'QTIP' to my team by the end of the month.
- Use 'Expectation Mountain' with every department head on every project.

**What do all of these examples have in common?**
- They are simple. You'll remember them.
- They are concrete. You have specific things to do.
- They are specific. You know exactly who is involved.

---

## How to Implement Your Action Plan

The QUESTION process leads to success with your personal action plan. It is designed to make sure your action plan works well. As you go through each letter in the process, write notes in each row, across from the corresponding step in the process. Use all the space available, and capture as much of your thinking as you can. You will want to refer back to this later. The more detail, the better.

## *Q:* "Question" your Action Plan.

Answer these questions to make sure your action plan is written out exactly the way you want it. If it's not quite right, with the help of these questions, re-phrase it. Write it over again in the 'Q' row, then move on to the next letter.

- Do I need to change any words to make it simple, concrete, specific?
- What part of this action plan is difficult for me?
- Is it really what I want to accomplish?

## *U:* Is it "Understandable?"

Can you predict the effect this action plan might have on you or others when you put it in place? Are you ready to embrace this change? Will you give it the time it needs to become a habit?

Consider these questions:
- Do I understand the benefits of this action plan?
- Do I understand the big picture and how hard this might be?
- If someone asked me to explain the reason behind my plan, could I?

In the 'U' row, write down at least one thought you'll want to come back to later.

---

## *E:* Represents "Evaluate"

How are you going to set up checks and balances, so you can see how the action plan is working for you? Let's write some down.

First, establish a near-term date to review your action plan and make sure it is working. Then continue to review the plan at regular intervals. This will keep your action plan front and center.

Evaluate your action plan by reviewing these questions:
- How often should you evaluate?
- Where can I document my reminders and evaluations?
- How am I specifically going to evaluate success?
- What will I do if I am not happy with the results?

---

## *S:* Ask "Is it Specific?"

Your action plan has to be precise. If the action plan is too ambiguous, too lofty, or too complex, your chances for success diminish. Make sure your plan is simple enough to tackle, yet measurable and challenging.

Consider these questions:
- Is the action plan, as written, specific enough?
- Can I start working on this right away?
- Will this action plan improve my coaching skills?

## *T:* Represents "Tricks"

Your action plan frequently includes coaching skills of which you will need to remind yourself. Develop 'tricks' that help you remember to use the skills and tools you are working on.

What kind of trick will help you remember what you are working on?

**Examples:**

| Action plan | Corresponding Trick |
|---|---|
| Use the 3-Sentence Rule at my weekly staff meetings. | Put three pencils on the table during every meeting. |
| Show I am listening to my boss by leaning in slightly when she talks. | Sit on the edge of the seat when I go into her office. |
| Use questions to help Lorie create solutions for the problems she brings me. | Put a question mark paperweight on my desk and leave it there permanently. |
| Get up and move away from my desk when direct reports are in my office. | Put the word 'push' over the top of the door so I can read it when someone walks into my office. Push away from the desk. |

## *I:* Stands for is it "Important" enough?

Do you see personal value in the plan you've made? If you don't, then re-write it or simply start a new action plan. If you don't believe this is important, then it will not happen.

Reflect on these questions:

- Will I think about it every day?
- Does it really make a difference?
- Do I care about it?

## *O:* Asks this question: Do you "Own" it?

Do you 'own' your action plan? Answer 'yes' to these questions and you do. Don't pursue an action plan you can't truly own and take responsibility for.

- Do I want this new behavior as part of my life?
- Do I want it badly enough to change?
- What will happen when I reach my goal?
- Do I truly believe in this action plan?

*N:* **reminds you to "Name" an accountability partner:**

Tackling something new, especially coaching can be difficult. It is possible to handle change completely on your own, but it's hard.

Identify an accountability partner. You will want a companion on your journey: someone who can continue to push you, challenge you, and support you. You will need someone who will be honest, frank, and tell you what you need to hear. When you ask the person you have selected, be specific about what you are asking them to do. Make sure you have someone who is willing to give you everything you need as your accountability partner. Find the right person and reach agreement.

Consider these questions as you select an accountability partner:

- Who can I share this with?
- Who will double-check to see that I am working on this?
- Who can be my cheerleader, while still holding me accountable?
- Who will be honest with me and give me the hard truths?

---

## What happens when you live out your Action Plan?

**Every action and every change will draw a reaction.** In Chapter Three, we talked about the changes you will create in others as you change your management style.

Everything you do as you develop your coaching skills is going to have ramifications. Why? Simply put, all behaviors are noticeable. They affect the people around you. When you change your behavior, people will react differently to you. Their perceptions about you might even change. Sometimes, a positive change in your behavior won't sit well with everyone. People may want the 'old you' to come back.

You have made a promise to yourself, in the form of an action plan. When you succeed with it, how might people react? Take a little time and write out both the positive and negative ways people around you might react to the changes they see.

Are you ready for all of this? Hang in there. Reactions, whether positive or negative, suggest that your new behavior is working. It is important that you spend time reflecting on this. Make time to evaluate, and then evaluate some more, as to how well your new approach is working. You can always fine tune, just don't let anything stop you from moving forward.

These are examples of ramifications we have seen as managers activate new behaviors or a new management style:

| Change | Ramification |
|---|---|
| Speak less in meetings, instead of talking too much. | People felt empowered and offered more opinions. I 'owned' fewer problems. |
| Connect with my people, instead of having my door closed all of the time. | New ideas from people I'd never heard from before. Attitudes with staff improved because of open door policy. |

You might think the ramifications of good communication would always be positive. Where that is usually true, you might be surprised to find that some people have a tough time with changes of any kind. They know you as you are today.

---

**Stories from the Summit:**

*Dan was the manager of an apartment leasing firm. He had a great relationship with Janet, his assistant. Dan told Janet everything. One of the issues Dan dealt with was his Vice Presidents hearing things before he could tell them personally.*

*Dan finally figured out that Janet was the one who told people. Dan stopped telling Janet things she didn't need to know. He no longer brought up anything that could get back to the Vice Presidents too early. One day, Janet asked: "What have you done with my Dan? I want him back." Janet did not react well to Dan's new approach at first, but it was for the best, and she did get used to it.*

---

You touch more people in the course of a day than you might think. Your new approach, as reflected in your action plan, can have far-reaching impact. More often than not, your people will receive the 'new you' positively.

If they are not ready for you to be different, give them time to adjust. They will. Who knows? You might very well change their behavior for the better, too.

Live out your action plan by using the 'QUESTION' process. Be clear on the ramifications that your new change is going to have on others. Hang in there. You can do this.

Spend the time you need. Put in the effort that your action plan deserves. Then, reap the rewards that come from it. Most of *being* is taking time to focus on goals and move constantly toward success.

---

You and your team will always have to get things done. There is nothing wrong with doing, but there is more.

BE... don't do. It sounds comfortable, and it is. When you listen, ask questions and stay centered, remarkable things happen. The people around you know you care. They start to care, too. You share a vision. Together, you work hard to make it real. You can do it naturally, with no stress, as you enjoy working together.

You're a leader. It's up to you to make this all possible for everyone. It's up to you. Use the model of the Sherpa Guide. Know your surroundings. Be a respected expert. Don't force things. People have to make the climb using their own skill and determination. All you can really do is unleash the best they have.

To set people free, you must *be* the best you can be.

*Be* in the moment.

*Be* at peace.

*Be.*

# Chapter Eight
## What You Need to Know: FAQs

You have taken on a new way of managing and a new way of leading. You have processes that help you get to the bottom of things and get things done.

With your action plan, you have both a proposition and a promise to never return to your old management style when dealing with business behaviors. With that, you have reached a new summit, a personal peak where performance comes more readily for you and your team.

The best way to help you on this journey is to share the questions we hear most frequently from the managers we work with, and give you our best answers. All of these questions have to do with this new coaching component of your job, and what it means to be a coaching leader.

- *What does it mean to be a successful coach? Will I know when I get there?*

A successful coach brings out the best in others and makes it easy for them to perform at their peak. When you have time to do what you want to do, when you are less stressed, when your team is happy and successful, you'll know you have arrived.

- *Why is it so important to be both a coach and a manager?*

People don't like being bossed around. They like to learn. To get people to be their best, you have to manage their skills and coach their behavior. If all you do is manage, your team's relationships will suffer. They might be successful, but they won't be happy. If all you do is coach, then you are probably not spending enough time on the bottom line. Your team will be happy, but they won't be as successful as they should.

- *Do I have to change who I am to be a coach?*

No, but you have to *be* in control of who you are. Focus on using the coaching tools and processes you have learned. Be aware of the ways your new behavior affects the people you work with. Know your own weaknesses. Understand your Why It Matters. You'll be the best you can be, without losing who you have always been.

- *How do I know I am coaching correctly?*

In the moment, you don't. Watch the results and practice, practice, practice. There is no such thing as perfect, or totally correct. Everyone who works for you is a work in progress. So are you. You'll get better with time, guaranteed.

- *How does helping them... help me?*

Sure, coaching helps the people who work for you. The biggest benefits will come to you. All of a sudden, you will have more time. You will 'own' fewer problems. You will be less stressed. Your job is an important part of your life, but it's not your whole life. Coaching will give you more time for life, while you and your team do the same amount of work, or more.

- *Is there a time when I shouldn't coach?*

Of course. Not every moment is a coaching moment. Instinctively, you'll know when to train, coach, consult or simply be a cheerleader. All of those approaches have value at the right time. Manage skills, coach behavior. When you need to coach, make sure you *are* coaching. Never let time be a deciding factor. Time invested now will be time saved in the long run.

- *How can I get in trouble as a coach?*

It's almost impossible. You are working with business behavior. If you sense that someone could use personal help, back away and connect them with your employee assistance program. If you understand your role as a coach and know where it ends it's almost impossible to do any harm.

- *What if I really don't want to coach one of my direct reports?*

Ask yourself: Is this person doing their job? Are they worth keeping? If they are, then spend time coaching. If not, be prepared to let people go every once in a while. The more you act as a coaching manager, the less you will have occasion to let someone go.

- *What will coaching do for me?*

You'll be a much better leader. You can tell people what you need, get instant understanding and true cooperation. You become an amazing communicator when you slow down to listen to your people. Coaching lets you *be* the total package.

## Afterword
## Are you ready to live like a coach?

**To be a coach, <u>live</u> like a coach.** You have learned how to *be*, instead of just *doing*. Being a coach isn't that hard, once you get some practice and optimize your own behavior. Coaching is more than a series of steps, a set of tools or a process. It means living like a coach.

**Use the 3-Sentence Rule with your family.** Practice listening skills with your family and friends. When you live like a coach, you act like a coach, and you know *when* to act like a coach. With all that, you will *be* a coach.

**When you stop owning things, you can BE.** Hear the words people say, and give those words to the person who truly owns them. Don't *do*... *be*.

**Asking questions allows you to BE.** When you ask great questions, you clarify and define what people need. You are not doing, you are being.

**When you follow the process for setting expectations:** communicate, commitment, consequences and coaching, you are not doing the work. You are making it possible for others to understand and do. *Be*, don't do.

**Using coaching moments keeps you from solving every problem.** Problem solving is doing. You are going to have to solve problems, at least some of them. It is part of your job, but you should not solve them *all*. You don't have to *do* all of the time. Know when to *be*, too!

You have the tools. You have the skills. You'll develop the behavior to *be* the best you can be. Do not dwell in the past; do not dream of the future. Concentrate the mind on the present moment.

May God bless your journey.

*Brenda Corbett*
*Judith Colemon*

# About the authors:

**A native of Canada, Brenda Corbett** has defined executive coaching and leadership development here in the US. Along with Judith Colemon, she wrote *The Sherpa Guide: Process-Driven Executive Coaching*, a book that provides clear methods and standards for executive coaching.

At Sherpa Coaching, based in Cincinnati, Corbett trains and certifies executive coaches using *The Sherpa Guide* as a text. She leads programs at The University of Georgia and the University of Pretoria in South Africa. The Sherpa certification is the only program endorsed by multiple universities, ten in all.

Corbett has trained and certified executive coaches for Stanley Black & Decker, Federal Express, Liz Claiborne, Toyota and US Bank, among others. Her degree comes from Waterloo, Canada's finest University.

---

**Judith Colemon** is an author and educator who trains and certifies executive coaches.

Along with Brenda Corbett, Colemon penned The Sherpa Guide: Process-Driven Executive Coaching, the world's most widely used textbook for coach training.

Ms. Colemon's work in executive coaching is based on experience as a CEO, for both a startup and an established institution. With her passion for leadership, she began coaching executives one-on-one nearly ten years ago.

She's still coaching, and she's a leading authority in the field. Colemon has trained coaches for Toyota, Liberty Mutual, Hershey and the National Cancer Institute. She continues certifying executive coaches at Penn State, the University of Georgia and Texas Christian University.

Ms. Colemon is a Cincinnati native and a graduate of the University of Dayton.

108